While Mortals Sleep

While Mortals Sleep

*Reading Phillips Brooks
through Twenty-First-Century Eyes*

EDITED BY
ROBERT D. FLANAGAN

Introduction by Ian S. Markham

☙PICKWICK *Publications* · Eugene, Oregon

WHILE MORTALS SLEEP
Reading Phillips Brooks through Twenty-First-Century Eyes

Copyright © 2025 Wipf and Stock Publishers. All rights reserved. Except for brief quotations in critical publications or reviews, no part of this book may be reproduced in any manner without prior written permission from the publisher. Write: Permissions, Wipf and Stock Publishers, 199 W. 8th Ave., Suite 3, Eugene, OR 97401.

Pickwick Publications
An Imprint of Wipf and Stock Publishers
199 W. 8th Ave., Suite 3
Eugene, OR 97401

www.wipfandstock.com

PAPERBACK ISBN: 979-8-3852-3666-4
HARDCOVER ISBN: 979-8-3852-3667-1
EBOOK ISBN: 979-8-3852-3668-8

Cataloguing-in-Publication data:

Names: Flanagan, Robert D., editor. | Markham, Ian S., introduction. | Roaf, Phoebe A., afterword.

Title: While Mortals Sleep : Reading Phillips Brooks through Twenty-First-Century Eyes / edited by Robert D. Flanagan ; introduction by Ian S. Markham.

Description: Eugene, OR: Pickwick Publications, 2025. | Includes bibliographical references.

Identifiers: ISBN 979-8-3852-3666-4 (paperback). | ISBN 979-8-3852-3667-1 (hardcover). | ISBN 979-8-3852-3668-8 (ebook).

Subjects: LCSH: Brooks, Phillips, 1835–1893. | Clergymen, American—19th century. | Episcopal Church—History. | Virginia Theological Seminary.

Classification: BX5995.B8 W35 2025 (paperback). | BX5995.B8 (ebook).

05/21/25

Publication of this work has been supported by a grant from the Historical Society of the Episcopal Church.

Scripture quotations marked NRSV are taken from the New Revised Standard Version Bible, copyright © 1989 the Division of Christian Education of the National Council of the Churches of Christ in the United States of America. Used by permission. All rights reserved.

From Brooks School to my doctorate, I dedicate this book to Frank D. Ashburn of Brooks School and to Barney Hawkins of my Virginia Theological Seminary doctorate.

"Be faithful unto death and may you have the blessed reward at the last 'well done good and faithful servant.'"

—Mary Ann Phillips's Letter to Phillips Brooks, October 12, 1859

Contents

Photos | ix

Acknowledgments | xi

Introduction | xiii
    Ian S. Markham

Contributors | xvii

1. So God Imparts to Human Hearts: Mary Ann Phillips's Influence on Phillips Brooks | 1
   Elaine B. Flanagan

2. In Thy Dark Streets: The Seminary Experience of Phillips Brooks | 16
   Robert D. Flanagan

3. Where Faith Holds Wide the Door: Phillips Brooks in Philadelphia | 34
   Rachel Wenner Gardner

4. How Still: The Participatory Poetry and Theology of "O Little Town of Bethlehem" | 52
   Karen Swallow Prior

5. Glory Breaks: Brooks's Influence on Trinity Church in the City of Boston | 71
   Cynthia E. Staples and Morgan S. Allen

6. The Great Glad Tidings Tell: The Relevance of Phillips Brooks for Contemporary Preaching | 86
   Ruthanna B. Hooke

Contents

7 Abide With Us: Brooks's Rise to the Bishop of Massachusetts | 104
 Robert D. Flanagan

8 The Everlasting Light: Phillips Brooks's Legacy at the Phillips Brooks House Association | 121
 Mary Catherine Curley

Afterword | 135
 The Rt. Rev. Phoebe A. Roaf

Photos

Mary Ann Phillips with infant Phillips Brooks (circa 1835) | 67

The Brooks family (1860) | 68

Phillips, Arthur, and John Cotton Brooks | 69

Phillips Brooks | 70

Acknowledgments

THIS BOOK IS A product of many conversations, vigorous research, quiet dedication, and the assistance of several key people. The editor and contributors are indebted to their openness, hospitality, and professionalism.

Beth Clark, Virginia Theological Seminary class of 2026, supported the project from its onset. Her assistance before and during the Phillips Brooks Conference at Virginia Theological Seminary in January 2024 was invaluable. We thank her for her commitment to the project and Phillips Brooks, her scholarly inquisitiveness, and amiable help.

Maria Dominguez Gray is Executive Director of the Phillips Brooks House Association and Harvard College class of 1955. She welcomed the opportunity to include PBHA's fabulous work inspired by the life of Phillips Brooks. Her effort brought a view of Phillips Brooks's legacy as a living presence, connecting outstanding students with the Boston area's people in need. We are thankful for the inclusion of the PBHA story and Maria's eagerness to bring an energetic view of Brooks. Phillips would likely be embarrassed by the attention his famous hymn has received but briming with pride at PBHA's quiet influence on Harvard students, the College, and the people of Boston.

Working with any library system, especially one as large as Harvard's, is daunting and navigating the necessary procedures and process to handle hundred-plus-year-old letters, sermons, photos, and notebooks is challenging. The editor and contributors appreciate the friendliness and professionalism of the Harvard Library Archives' staff and in particular reference librarian, Zoë Hill. Phillips's family and their close relationships spring to life as we read their hand-written letters, his passionate preaching felt alive, and his youthful notebooks exhibited Brooks's emotional state at seminary

Acknowledgments

and his feistiness about political issues. We are grateful for Harvard's continued custodianship of the Phillips Brooks archive material.

The Historical Society of the Episcopal Church assisted the editor in the closing months of manuscript writing. Its grant allowed for the editor to make one last Cambridge trip to examine Brooks's episcopal election and shift through the blind praise of Phillips from the controversy's facts. The Society's support of historical research is invaluable to bringing projects as this one to fruition.

The Pickwick Publications editorial team stands tall in the publishing industry. The editor and contributors are grateful to the team for its support of the project and its assistance with creating a beautiful book and a valuable resource.

Introduction

Ian S. Markham

PERHAPS HE WAS AMERICA'S most famous religious public figure in the 1800s. Phillips Brooks (1835–1893) had an extraordinary profile. Although the Episcopal Church was smaller than the Methodist and Roman Catholic traditions, it was deeply influential. Several of the founding fathers were Episcopalian: George Washington, James Madison, and James Monroe. Many of the original families that came from England were Episcopalians. Brooks was an Episcopal priest who became a bishop. He was a hymnwriter, an extraordinary preacher, and a person deeply in conversation with the challenges of his time. He was an opponent of slavery and argued and worked for its abolition. His education was exceptional and included the Boston Latin School, Harvard University, and Virginia Theological Seminary. Almost all of us know his famous Christmas carol, "O Little Town of Bethlehem." And many of us know his acclaimed sermon on the death of Abraham Lincoln. Perhaps we also know that he became the Rector of Trinity Church, in Boston (the most significant pulpit in the country at the time) and working with Henry Hobson Richardson created a stunning church. This is a collection of essays that explores every aspect of Brooks's life—from his mother's influence, his education, his service in Philadelphia and Boston, his preaching, his hymnody, his disputed election to the episcopacy, and his legacy.

In many ways, this book is seeking to push back on certain trends in the academy. The assumption is that an individual can make a difference. Many of us have absorbed a loosely Marxist attitude to life: we assume that in the end in the end we are all cogs in an economic and sociologically-driven machine. The sociological forces, which are shaped by economics, are the ones that matter. An individual person does not really make a difference. Those with economic power will triumph, save for the *tipping point* when finally, the less powerful group gets to push back. The Church however wants to disagree with this analysis. Granted economic forces are strong, but a God-inspired individual can have a massive impact and really transcend the economic and sociological forces operating.

THE ANGLICAN APPROACH TO HISTORY

For Anglicans, a *saint* can make a difference. In the ecology of faith, there is no inevitability about the future. And just one person living sensitive to the demands of the moment can make a difference. Church is in the business of letting God transform lives into agents of the kingdom. One person can make a difference.

This is not to say that we do not recognize the complex dynamic of history. In an Anglican historical methodology, there are four parameters that shape our understanding of history. The first two are sin and grace. The third is evil. And the last one is the existence of saints. Let us examine these four parameters.

The witness of the Church always says that every age is made up of sin and grace. Every human being is fallen. We are all shaped by misguided values and attitudes of our time. Motivations are often mixed. And simultaneously, grace is found in the imago dei (the image of God), which is part of every human being. We all have the potential for good. And we often surprise ourselves as a simple act of kindness has ripples that we could not foresee.

The Church also recognizes that there are certain moments in history when evil appears very strong. A good illustration is the Nazi regime in Germany who marched innocent lives into a concentrated camp, many of whom were gassed to death. Chattel slavery is a comparable sin; to treat a human person as property that, economically, is equivalent to livestock is a heinous sin.

The Church also teaches that certain human lives are worthy of study and imitation. Anglicans believe that a *saint* was an exceptional human being who has lived a holy life. Often saints are people who overcame adversity. Their faith was especially admirable. And they exhibited the Christians virtues in ways that we should aspire to emulate.

Introduction

These four parameters—sin, grace, evil, and saints—should guide the Christian study of history. Sin and grace inevitably pervade his life. In the chapter by Cynthia Staples and Morgan Allen, we learn that those working on the construction of Trinity Church were enmeshed in the world of enslaved people. It was inevitable that his circle included people associated with the evil institution of slavery—so, evil gets in too. As Elaine Flanagan shows Brooks is a person of privilege, enjoying an extraordinary education and, for his time, an affluent lifestyle. Yet the grace can be seen in the way in which he became a priest and a pastor, which is captured by Rachel Wenner Gardner's chapter about Brooks in Philadelphia. His experience at Seminary, as Robert Flanagan shows, reinforced his opposition to the institution of slavery. Brooks had a moral insight that many at the Seminary could not see. The poetry of Brooks is beautifully captured by Karen Swallow Prior. He was an extraordinary preacher, which according to Ruthanna Hooke, has insights from which those in homiletics can continue to learn. And as a candidate for bishop, explains Robert Flanagan, he combined a *liberalism* with a deep commitment to Christ. He brought a rich, faithful Gospel of love to his parishioners and to his diocese. All of this is grace. It is a sadness, as Bishop Roaf in the afterword notes, that he was not granted a longer tenure as Bishop; it might have been even more transformative.

The Episcopal Church has chosen to designate Phillips Brooks a *saint*. He has his day; he is remembered on January 23. The day is technically a lesser feast and fast. So, there are seven principal feasts in the Episcopal Church—Easter Day, Ascension Day, Pentecost, Trinity Sunday, All Saints' Day, Christmas Day, and Epiphany. Then the Episcopal Church talks of *major holy days*—the feasts of our Lord, all feasts of apostles, and other key occasions). Phillips Brooks slots underneath these occasions. It is a *significant day*.

This book is not an exercise in hagiography. It is a critical and respectful engagement with his life. We will journey through his childhood; we will engage with the different seasons of his life—seminarian, rector, bishop; we will explore his skills as a hymn writer and preacher; and we will examine his legacy.

AN OFFERING TO UNDERSTANDING THE PAST

Virginia Theological Seminary organized the conference that underpins this collection of essays. As a Seminary, we were founded in 1823. Phillips

Introduction

Brooks was a student at the Seminary. We have been marking our Bicentenary. Part of our work was to take a good, long, hard look at our past. We are very conscious that much of our past is grounded in horrendous sin. We are also aware that this sinful institution did produce some amazing graduates who, on balance, were voices of good in this world of ours.

We take January 23—Phillips Brooks's day—very seriously. We believe that this life is a life worthy of study and emulation. Sin and evil are still present and should not be overlooked. We trust that this collection of essays will continue to help the Church think about how best to engage with our complex past. Phillips Brooks is a light in the darkness in so many ways. For his witness, we are grateful.

Contributors

MORGAN S. ALLEN, MDiv, is the twenty-first Rector of Trinity Church in the City of Boston.

MARY CATHERINE CURLEY is a writer and Alumna of Phillips Brooks House Association, Harvard College Class of 2010. Her writing has appeared in the *Kenyon Review* and the *Hopkins Review*, among others.

ELAINE B. FLANAGAN, MAT, is an early childhood educator and for five years taught in a school in Andover, Massachusetts, driving daily past Phillips Brooks's statue on the North Andover green. Her husband and two adult children are graduates of the Brooks School (North Andover, MA).

ROBERT D. FLANAGAN, DMin, is a writer, Episcopal priest, graduate of Brooks School and Virginia Theological Seminary. His books include the *Courage to Thrive* series and *The Letters of an Unexpected Mystic*.

RACHEL WENNER GARDNER, MDiv, is the fourteenth Rector at The Church of the Holy Trinity, Philadelphia (Rittenhouse Square). Phillips Brooks was the second Rector at Holy Trinity.

RUTHANNA B. HOOKE, PhD, is Professor of Homiletics at Virginia Theological Seminary and also Program Director of "The Preaching Congregations Initiative." Her publications include *Sacramental Presence: An Embodied Theology of Preaching* and *Transforming Preaching*.

IAN S. MARKHAM, PhD, is Dean and President of the Virginia Theological Seminary.

Contributors

Karen Swallow Prior, PhD, is an independent scholar, speaker, and monthly columnist for Religion News Service. Her books include *On Reading Well: Finding the Good Life in Great Books* and *The Evangelical Imagination: How Stories, Images, and Metaphors Created a Culture in Crisis*.

Rt. Rev. Phoebe Roaf is the Bishop of the Episcopal Diocese of West Tennessee.

Cynthia E. Staples is the historian at Trinity Church in the City of Boston.

1

So God Imparts to Human Hearts
Mary Ann Phillips's Influence on Phillips Brooks

Elaine B. Flanagan

MORNING PRAYERS HAD BEEN said, and the six Brooks boys had eaten a hearty breakfast before departing for school. Phillips, William, and George Brooks headed off to the prestigious Boston Latin School, and the younger three Brooks boys attended Miss Capen's school or the local public elementary school. They were too young to attend the Boston Latin School, which started at age eleven. It was a typical weekday morning during the school year in the Brooks's home in the 1840s and 1850s.

A BRAHMIN LIFE

On this weekday morning, Mary Ann Phillips Brooks readied herself for her weekly Bible study at St. Paul's Episcopal Church. Other women joined her, many of whom were part of a class of people known as the *Boston Brahmin*. The Brahmin were the economically privileged and the social, political, and intellectually elite Bostonians of their time. The Bible study kept them current on the church's foreign missions, and they also read classical and current literature, which were acceptable ways for these women to spend their time.

Mary Ann and her husband, Willliam, were raising their family in Beacon Hill, the Brahmin family neighborhood. They resided on Chauncey Street, their third home since moving to the neighborhood. Their growing family demanded more space prompting their moves around Beacon Hill. The Chauncy Street home was comfortable, and Mary Ann employed two Irish domestics to help her run her bustling home. Even with the help, Mary Ann and William led quieter lives than their socially-active neighbors, spending their evenings at home with their boys.

A HOUSE FULL OF BOYS

Mary Ann's days were chockful of activity and parental duties. Once her six boys returned home from school, they usually played outside, but never after dark. The Brooks boys did not engage in formal sports, but like boys their age, enjoyed skating and sledding on the Boston Commons during the winter, for example. They spent summers at the Brooks family homestead in Andover, where the boys engaged in hours of daily outdoor play, like riding a neighbors "borrowed" cart downhill until they crashed it into a barn. Back at their Beacon Hill home, during the school year, they gathered in the back parlor after dinner. There, the older boys would finish their homework and read. Conversations often revolved around what they had learned in school, and Mary Ann and her husband welcomed their opinions on various current events and topics. The boys all retired to their beds by nine where Mary Ann would share a Bible story with them, and together said evening prayers.

The only career option for Mary Ann Phillips Brooks, an affluent white woman living in Massachusetts in the early nineteenth century, was being a mother, a role Mary Ann Phillips Brooks took very seriously. She was utterly devoted to her six children's physical, emotional, and spiritual development. Mary Ann Phillips Brooks had an intense love for and devotion to her family. Her dedication to her family, her deep faith, her selflessness, and her family history uniquely steeped in the education and religious life of its time, helped shaped the man Phillips Brooks.

SOCIAL AND CULTURAL INFLUENCES ON THE FAMILY

The culture of the United States today has shifted dramatically since the days that Mary Ann Phillips Brooks and her husband, William Gray

Brooks, raised their six boys in Boston. Education had previously been the responsibility of parents at home, and for the wealthy, private tutors often assisted with a child's educational development. Now it was available to the masses via public schools. Education had moved out of the house and into the public-school classroom. In the mid-1800s Boston, public schools now joined religious institutions and parents in shaping children's emotional and spiritual lives.

Mary Ann focused much of her attention on her sons' education. She educated her six sons at home until age five when she sent them to Miss Capen. Phillips Brooks, like his brothers, entered The Boston Latin School at eleven, graduating at the age of sixteen. Although her sons had left home for advanced academics, Mary Ann remained the force behind the formation of their religious and spiritual lives. She would continue to be the primary force, shaping her children's faith and values throughout their lives.

Despite shifting cultural and societal tides, parents today share similar goals for their children and want to instill comparable foundational values in their children. If Mary Ann Phillips Brooks were alive today, she would be like many parents who raise their children with core religious and ethical values. Three Pew Research Center surveys of 3757 parents of children under the age of eighteen, conducted between 2015 and 2020, examined the importance of passing on their religious and political views to their children and yielded the following results:

- Thirty-five percent of parents surveyed said it was extremely important that their children share their religious views.
- Sixteen percent of parents surveyed said it was extremely important that their children share their political views.
- Both religious and political views were less important than passing along other values, such as being honest, ethical, hardworking, and ambitious.[1]

Religious and educational institutions, make-up of the family unit, and women's roles in society have changed dramatically since Phillips Brooks's childhood days. Still, the desire of parents like Mary Ann Phillips Brooks to impart their religious views and values to their children remains an essential facet of parenting today.

---

1. Minkin and Horowitz, "Parenting."

In a letter written on March 11, 1867, to her son Phillips Brooks, then Rector of Holy Trinity Church in Philadelphia, Pennsylvania, Mary Ann expressed her zeal and desire for her sons to have a deep faith in Jesus Christ. She was singularly focused on raising her sons to know the Gospels, experience an inner conversion, and ultimately accept Jesus Christ as their Savior. Her Christian vocation was to raise her six children to become Christians. She writes:

> My dearest Philly,
> ... And now Philly, I know you will rejoice with me that Johnny has become so interested in religion and is intending to become confirmed. I cannot tell you how happy it makes me and how grateful that my earnest prayers, that this my youngest one should not be left out of the Fold, have been so graciously heard. You know dear Philly how anxious I have been for all of you. So you can or will judge my joy, yet you cannot judge, for none but a Mother can know the yearning she feels for her child's salvation. Oh, how I thank God for it![2]

In this letter Mary Ann Phillips Brooks refers to her youngest child, John Cotton, named after the Rev. John Cotton, a prominent minister and theologian of the Massachusetts Bay Colony and a distant Brooks family relative. John Cotton Brooks will become the fourth of Mary Ann's six sons to become an ordained Episcopal minister.

THE PHILLIPS FAMILY OF ANDOVER, MASSACHUSETTS

Mary Ann Phillips Brooks was born in Andover, Massachusetts, on March 17, 1808, to John Phillips and Lydia Phillips. The Phillips family was prominent in Massachusetts and southern New Hampshire. The Phillipses were known for their commitment and contributions to the towns where they lived. Their contributions extended beyond the educational and religious institutions that they helped to found and support; many members of the Phillips family served on local town councils and were elected officials. As a child, Mary Ann witnessed the importance of service to others, which was exemplified in the lives of many of her family members. From that, Mary Ann grew determined for her children to serve others. She expressed

---

2. Mary Ann Phillips Brooks, to Phillips Brooks, 12 October 1859, Phillips Brooks Papers, bMS AM 2022, box 1, folder 21, Houghton Library, Harvard University.

it tenderly in her numerous letters to Phillips and his brothers throughout their lives.

In her letter of October 12, 1859 to Phillips, she wrote:

> My Dearest Son,
>
> ... I enjoyed your last letter to your father very much. You told him so much about your parish, and all that you are doing, and you seem to be prospering so much—and you seem to feel interested in your work and how can you help it, it is an honour. How happy to be allowed to preach Christ's blessed gospel to poor perishing souls.
>
> Oh Phillips be faithful to them and your Master—and I believe you are, from the interest of your people seem to feel in your preaching and especially from your choice of texts. I admire them they are so full of Christ. Philly, I need not ask if you are happy, I know you are, you must be. Be faithful unto death and may you have the blessed reward at the last 'well done good and faithful servant.'

On MaryAnn's paternal side of the family, there was a long line of influential preachers spanning several generations, beginning with Reverend George Phillips. Reverend George Phillips left England with his family seeking religious freedom. His ship anchored in Salem, Massachusetts, on June 12, 1630. Reverend George Phillips settled with his family in Watertown, Massachusetts, near Boston, where he began to preach. He preached at the parish in Watertown until the time of his death. Each generation of the Phillips family subsequently produced ordained ministers. The Reverend Samuel Phillips, born in 1690, helped establish the South Parish in Andover, Massachusetts and served there for 60 years beginning in 1711 and ending with his death in 1771. The death of Reverend Samuel Phillips marks the break for several generations of ordained ministers in the Phillips family line. The line of ordained ministers was broken briefly, but "the underlying religious spirit" still existed in the family as they endeavored for new livelihoods.[3]

John Phillips, the father of Mary Ann Phillips, was born in 1776, shortly after the death of his great-grandfather, the renowned Andover minister, Reverend Samuel Phillips. John was raised in Andover, attending South Parish, where generations of his family had worshipped, and where generations rest in the church's cemetery.

---

3. Feuss, *Old New England School*, 5.

In 1778, Phillips Brooks's great-grandfather, Samuel Phillips, Jr. founded Phillips Andover Academy in Andover with funds from several Phillips family members. Less than two years later other Phillips family members established the Phillips Academy in Exeter, New Hampshire. The Andover Theological Seminary was founded in 1808 with financial contributions from Samuel Abbott, a successful Boston businessman, and contributions from several members of the Phillips family. The seminary was housed on the Phillips Andover Academy campus, it was the first educational institution in the United States to offer graduate degrees.

Mary Ann Phillips, the daughter of John and Lydia Gorham Phillips, was raised in the town of Andover, Massachusetts, with its renowned educational and religious institutions. It was where she married William Gray Brooks. She and William would go on to raise their six sons in Boston with summers spent at the family homestead in Andover.[4]

THE BROOKS FAMILY'S PLACE IN NEW ENGLAND'S HISTORY

Phillips Brooks's paternal side of the family had fewer ordained ministers than the maternal side. Despite the lesser numbers, they influenced generations of Brooks family members and New Englanders. The Reverend John Cotton was born in 1585 in England, left England amidst persecution, and arrived in New England in September 1633. John Cotton and Thomas Hooker were the two ministers who established First Parish in Boston in the Massachusetts Bay Colony. John Cotton was described as an intellectual with an "evangelical spirit."[5] He became the spokesman for the new church polity known as Congregationalism.[6] John Cotton had a large volume of written works, including a short catechism for children entitled "Spiritual Milk for Boston Babes," it was the first children's book written by an American. Around 1701, the volume was incorporated into The New England Primer, it remained a part of that publication for 150 years.[7]

---

4. Andover, Massachusetts was split into two towns, Andover and North Andover, in 1855. The Phillips Brooks home sits in the Town of North Andover today.

5. Emerson, *John Cotton*, 35.

6. Ziff, *John Cotton*, 96.

7. Cotton, John (1646). Royster, Paul (ed.) "Milk for Babes. . ."(http://digitalcommons.unl.edu/etas/18/) *Electronic Texts in American Studies*. University of Nebraska, Lincoln Libraries.

One can see the similarities between the Brooks and Phillips families with regard to the role of religion and education in family life. These two families shaped the educational and religious culture of New England. If DNA could dictate career choice, it is easy to see why Phillips Brooks's first career, although short lived, would be one of a teacher at his alma mater, The Boston Latin School, followed by a second career as an ordained minister.

MARY ANN PHILLIPS, A TEACHER AND STUDENT

Mary Ann Phillips was raised in a family that valued religious tradition, faith, and rigorous academics. Her deep faith, along with her thirst and curiosity for expanding her own theological knowledge, are the foundation of her family's life. There was no higher calling for Mary Ann than to raise her children in a home filled with Christian love and warmth, in a place that provided a solid religious foundation for them. Mary Ann created a rich home life for her children with daily Bible reading and prayers. Prayers were said in the morning before school and again in the evening before bed. The Brooks children's spiritual formation and religious education began in the home with Mary Ann taking the lead in this area of her children's development. The church pew was an extension of the home and, thus, the other place where Mary Ann's sons' young minds and hearts were shaped and nurtured. Mary Ann was determined, diligent, and singularly focused on sharing her faith with her children. The family attended church services twice on Sundays, followed by hymn singing at home on Sunday evenings. Starting at an early age, each child in the family would memorize a hymn to be shared with the family. It is said that by the time Phillips Brooks entered Virginia Seminary he had memorized nearly two hundred hymns.[8]

Mary Ann attended numerous Bible studies at St. Paul's in Boston where she strengthened her faith and deepened her understanding of religious matters. She returned home after her studies better equipped to develop and nurture a Christian way of life for her children. She lovingly and warmly imparted her ever-growing understanding of religion and faith to her children. Mary Ann was both a student and a teacher in these matters. She was a woman of actions and words when faith was involved.

Mary Ann Phillips Brooks educated her children at home until about the age of 5, at which point the home education was supplemented by the services of a local female teacher, Miss Capen. After completing his studies

8. Harp, *Brahmin Prophet*, 13.

with Miss Capen, Phillips attended a local public grammar school before entering The Boston Latin School at age 11. He graduated from Boston Latin at age 16 and entered Harvard College. Mary Ann's attention to her children's growth and well-being did not stop when they went to college or seminary.

PHILLIPS'S TIME AT VIRGINIA SEMINARY

Phillips left Boston at almost twenty-one to study at Virginia Seminary in Alexandria, Virginia. Mary Ann wrote extensively to Phillips while he was away at seminary, expressing her affection, her concern for his well-being, and a curiosity about his studies. Her tender and loving correspondence with him showed her parental anxiety and deep concern for Phillips' well-being. It was not easy for her to have one of her sons so far away from home. She wanted Phillips to always feel a part of her home despite the distance that separated them. She had not, in any way, relinquished her parental duties despite Phillips's age and distance from her while at seminary.

In a letter to Phillips at seminary on October 20, 1857, she writes:[9]

> My Dear Philly,
> I am thinking of you continually and we cannot be done missing you, and it is so cheering to get news of you. I wish I could look into your room and see if you look comfortable, and how you have arranged your clothes . . . I hope you will find some pleasant friends amongst the new students. Also I hope you will improve this pleasant weather to walk a good deal and enjoy this beautiful weather . . . Have you written to Georgey since you left us? I have the good news to tell you that he is intending to come home soon . . . The thought of having him home is delightful, and he seems very happy at the thought of seeing us again. Father seems very glad to get him home again soon. Write again soon and tell us all about yourself and what you are doing in your studies this year. You don't know how much we think and talk of you and desire your well doing in every respect. Keep very near to your Saviour, dear Philly, and remember the sacred vows that are upon you, and you will surely prosper. Good night my dear Philly, and pleasant dreams. Whether waking or sleeping, never forget.
> Your ever loving Mother.

---

9. bMS AM 2022, box 1, folder 21.

So God Imparts to Human Hearts

On January 11, 1858, after a difficult Christmas without all her children at home, Mary Ann responded to Phillips's Christmas Eve 1857 letter from Alexandria, Virginia.[10]

> My Dear Philly,
> I thank you for your letter; it is a treasure to me, it is so full of love and kindness. It tells us all we want to know, that you realize your parents' deep interest in you and that you promise us the richest reward you can give us, that of bringing us honor in after life. And also you have convinced us that you have a warm and kind heart, and that your heart is in your profession. Not that I have ever doubted it, for I have always felt you are too sincere and too true hearted to dare undertake a holy calling except with your whole heart; but I have sometimes wished you would make it doubly sure to me, by assuring me of it yourself, and I have felt you owed it to yourself to do so. But, my dear Philly, this letter satisfies me entirely on that point, and I cannot tell you the delight it gives us. Father almost shed tears as he read it.[11]

Mary Ann Phillips Brooks loved her sons deeply. Her letters have a gracious tone to them. It was the tone of a parent who very much loved their children and missed them when they were outside the home. Despite the pain this may have caused Mary Ann, she still encouraged her sons on their vocations, wherever it may take them.

In her letter to Phillips during his final year at Virginia Seminary, Mary Ann Phillips Brooks wrote on February 14, 1859:[12]

> My dearest Phillips,
> I hope you are feeling well Phillips, do exercise and do your clothes hold out, make no doubt they should need a stitch, I should gladly give them. Do you not long to see your little chamber again? The pictures remain just as you left them and how they remind me of you and . . . many are the prayers I offer up to you in that room.
> Philly we all long to see you home again, all the boys are doing very well.
> Think of us as we do you, dear Philly, very often—write to us very soon, everything about yourself.
> Your loving and devoted, Mother

---

10. bMS AM 2022, box 1, folder 21.
11. Allen, *Phillips Brooks*, 1:212.
12. bMS AM 2022, box 1, folder 21.

MARY ANN TAKES A BOLD STANCE

There is no doubt of the deep love and affection Mary Ann Phillips Brooks had for her son Phillips and his brothers. Mary Ann not only desired to pass on her religious views; she felt it was her responsibility to do so and a commitment she took very seriously. Her desire to get her sons' religious upbringing right caused her to take a bold religious stance. Mary Ann stepped away from the faith of her Congregational ancestors and chose the Episcopal Church to raise Phillips and his brothers.

While raising her young family in Boston, Mary Ann Phillips Brooks attended the First Church on Chauncey Place, a parish whose members included many Boston Brahmin families. One of the founders of First Parish was the Reverend John Cotton, a distant relative of Mary Ann's husband, William Gray Brooks. Mary Ann sat faithfully in the pews every Sunday with her growing family, listening attentively to the preaching of First Church's pastor, Dr. Frothingham. A controversy and ultimately a schism had been brewing and growing in Congregational churches across the small towns and villages in Massachusetts. A movement known as Unitarianism was on the rise. Pastors and parishioners were choosing sides, Unitarian or Trinitarian. Mary Ann sought out a new place to worship with her family. Her husband, William Gray Brooks, was reluctant to leave First Parish, but ultimately joined her as a member of the Episcopal Church. For Mary Ann Phillips Brooks, born and raised a Trinitarian Congregationalist, leaving the Congregational Church, a church in which her family was deeply involved, was no easy matter of the heart and soul.

At the time, there were three Episcopal Parishes in Boston: Christ Church (Old North Church), Trinity Church, and St. Paul's Church. Through Mary Ann's contact with Dr. John Stone, the Rector of St. Paul's, she began to learn about the Evangelical or Low Church School. What followed for Mary Ann was a period of self-education. She learned about the Episcopal Church through numerous conversations with Dr. Stone. She studied the Prayer Book and learned about church polity. She dove deep into her study of the Episcopal Church with Dr. Stone as her guide. She was concerned about the baptism of her older children, which included Phillips, by Dr. Frothingham of First Parish. She raised this concern with Dr. Stone. He addressed her concerns and assured her that the baptisms should stand since the children had not been baptized into any particular form of Christianity. After a period of reflection and education, Mary Ann decided that she could join the Episcopal Church. She was able to do so without feeling as though she had abandoned the faith of her ancestors. She and her sister Susan Phillips were admitted into the Episcopal Church in 1839. Mary Ann's husband, William Gray Brooks, in his journal entry of October 18, 1839, described this transition:

> We have made an important movement this month so far as the change of our place of worship. We now have attended the Rev. Dr. Frothingham's church in Chauncey Place since we were married, just six years; but wife was never much pleased with Mr. F's liberal style of preaching, and after a good deal of consideration and reflection we concluded to change, and we have got a pew at St. Paul's (Episcopalian), where Rev. Dr. Stone officiates. For myself, I feel attached to the Unitarian Church, having been brought up to that doctrine; but at the same time I cannot say I have so much repugnance to the Orthodox sect as many have; the example of one of the best mothers would forbid it. Being, therefore, as I myself say, indifferent, I gave up my inclinations and prejudices for my old place of worship to gratify that of my wife. Certain it is that women make religion more a matter of conscience and the heart than men do. On many accounts I regretted leaving Dr. Frothingham's church.[13]

Despite William Brooks's hesitation at leaving First Parish, he began attending services at St. Paul's. On May 30, 1847, at age forty-four, he was confirmed by Bishop Eastburn at St. Paul's. Shortly after his confirmation, the church's Rector Dr. Stone departed St. Paul's, and Dr. Vinton became the church's next Rector. Dr. Vinton would become a close and influential friend of the Brooks family in the years to come.

A CLOSE FAMILY FRIEND AND MENTOR

Mary Ann's enthusiasm to impart her religious views to her children never diminished despite their ages and distance from her. She did everything in her capacity to expand her theological education in hopes that, in some way, it helped her sons develop a deep faith and a strong religious identity. Mary Ann attended numerous Bible studies led by Dr. Vinton at the family's new church, where he would explain doctrine and comment on the Epistles or the Gospel. His teachings enriched her spiritual life. In turn, she shared this knowledge with her children.

---

13. Allen, *Phillips Brooks*, 1:42.

Mary Ann relied on Dr. Vinton to help form and nurture her sons' religious and spiritual lives as they grew into young men. Mary Ann's deep yearning for her sons to be part of the fold led her to ask Dr. Vinton to write a letter of encouragement to her oldest sons. In his lengthy letter dated August 28, 1848, to William, Phillips, and George Brooks, Dr. Vinton wrote:

> . . . I have indeed almost unbounded confidence in the efficacy of a parent's prayers. I believe it clings to the life of a young man and follows him where he least expects it. The answer to such prayer seems omnipotent as it is wholesome.
>
> I know how earnestly such prayer has been offered for you, and therefore I am very hopeful. Still as you are free agents it is in your power to frustrate its blessing and it is the peculiar temptation of young men that they do not feel its need. If there be any one disposition of mind which I would wish you to cherish and cultivate most of all, it is that of dependence upon God.

The letter continues with advice regarding regular prayer and Bible study habits. It concluded:

> My prayer and hope for you are that I may see you at an early period consecrating yourselves to God in the open membership of his Church, showing that you are not ashamed of Him, and that you have experienced his renewing Grace. . . . May it be my joy at last, my dear young friends, to meet you at the right hand of our Saviour is the earnest prayer of your affectionate friend and pastor.
> Alex'r H Vinton[14]

In his letter to the oldest Brooks boys, Dr. Vinton acknowledged how powerfully Mary Ann, her husband, and Dr. Vinton had prayed for them. Mary Ann had a powerful ally in Dr. Vinton. Dr. Vinton mentored Phillips during his years at Virginia Seminary and later in his life as an ordained priest.

Mary Ann continued to send letters to her beloved son Phillips in the years following his graduation from seminary. Her letters expressed her affection for him and offered him encouragement in his ministry. Her letters contained glimpses into home life in Boston. She constantly reminded Phillips and his brothers that they were always in her thoughts and prayers. She remained dedicated to Phillips despite the distance that separated them. Phillips had Mary Ann's unwavering support and love during his entire life.

---

14. Allen, *Life and Letters*, 1:56.

So God Imparts to Human Hearts

On March 11, 1867, his mother wrote to Phillips, now Rector at Holy Trinity Church in Philadelphia:[15]

> . . . dear Philly, I do not know how to speak of your own work, it is a continued and increasing source of pleasure and delights to me, to thank God for you, for all you are and all you are doing for others. I pray Him to continue to help and bless you in your holy work. Oh, how continually God has blessed me in my children.

THE IMPACT OF LOVE AND FAITH

Mary Ann expressed numerous times in her letters to Phillips her gratitude to God that her children were faithful Christians serving God and their fellow citizens. There is no way to quantitatively measure the impact that Mary Ann's love, faith, and devotion to her family had on the development of Phillips and his brothers. She brought her deep faith, which she had cultivated from a young age, and further developed as a woman into the daily life of her home. She made this faith the foundation of the Brooks household. She was not only a woman of words but a woman of action. She took a bold stance regarding religion when she stepped away from the church of her ancestors and chose to raise her family in the Episcopal Church. This determined, brave, and faith-filled woman raised Phillips Brooks. Phillips was encouraged by and enveloped by the love of his mother his entire life.

PHILLIPS REFLECTS ON HIS MOTHER'S LIFE

Mary Ann Phillips Brooks died at seventy-two on February 1, 1880. Phillips was at his mother's bedside at the time of her passing. In the weeks following her death, we once again see the power and intensity of the love Mary Ann had for her children; this time, it is in the letters that Phillips wrote to family and friends in the days and weeks after his mother's death. Phillips wrote to a family friend, Dr. Weir Mitchell:

> My Mother has been the centre of all happiness of my life. Thank God she is not less my pride and treasure now.

---

15. bMS AM 2022, box 1, folder 21

To Mr. Cooper:

> I did not know I could ever be so much like a child again, but tonight the world seems very desolate and lonely. All my life I have feared and dreaded what has come this week. And now that she is with God, I seem to know for the first time how pure and true and self-sacrificing all her earthly life has been. Surely with all these that have gone before it will not be hard to go to Him when our time comes.

And to another friend, he writes:

> The happiest part of my happy life has been my Mother, and with God's help she will be more to me than ever. The sense of God and his love has grown ever clearer in the midst of all this sadness and bereavement.[16]

A parent's love and influence on a child's development cannot be measured. The home she created for her children was built on a foundation of faith and was filled with love and encouragement. She prayed to God for her children's salvation and for their futures in service to Him. It was Mary Ann's deep yearning that her children would know the depth of her love for them and that faith in Christ should be the guiding force in their lives. Her correspondence with Phillips and his brothers, as well as entries in her journals, showed that she believed God had answered her prayers.

MARY ANN'S THOUGHTS

Among some papers found after Mary Ann's death were the following personal notes:[17]

> September 28, 1862, Sunday evening. What a happy blessed day this has been to me! My dear George for whom I have prayed and longed and agonized for so many years, has today confessed his Saviour in Trinity Church at the age of twenty-three, before he leaves us for war. My desires and prayers have been granted. My eyes have seen the blessed sight, so ardently longed for. I want never to lose the vivid impression of that beautiful scene. I will never cease throughout Eternity to praise Him for this last great mercy, and for all the wonderful works he has done in my family. Four of my dear children are now safe in his Fold, and oh, may the

---

16. Allen, *Life and Letters*, 2:252.
17. Allen, *Life and Letters*, 1:422.

dear remaining ones be speedily brought in! And for this, and all this goodness I will praise his blessed name forever.

Another note, written several years earlier concerning Phiilips, was found in her possessions after her death.

> Sunday, July 12, 1857, This has been a most happy day in which I have witnessed the Confirmation of my dear son Phillips, aged twenty-one, at Dorchester.
>
> I will thank God forever that He has answered my lifelong prayers in making him a Christian and his servant in ministry.
>
> Oh, how happy this makes me! May God continue to bless my dear boy and make him a burning and shining light in His service.

Mary Ann Phillips Brooks, with God's help, raised a man who became a burning and shining light in the world.

BIBLIOGRAPHY

Albright, Raymond W. *Focus on Infinity: A Life of Phillips Brooks*. New York: Macmillan, 1961.

Allen, Alexander. *Life and Letters of Phillips Brooks*. Vol. III. New York: Dutton, 1901.

———. *Phillips Brooks 1835–1893, Memories of His Life with Extracts from His Letters and Notebooks*. New York: Dutton, 1907.

Emerson, Everett. *John Cotton*. New York: Wayne, 1990.

Feuss, Claude Moore. *An Old New England School: A History of Phillips Academy Andover*. Boston: Houghton Mifflin, 1917.

Harp, Gillis J. *Brahmin Prophet, Phillips Brooks and the Path of Liberal Protestantism*. Lanham, MD: Rowand & Littlefield, 2003.

Lawrence, William. *The Life of Phillips Brooks*. New York: Harper, 1930.

Minkin, Rachel, and Menasce Horowitz. "Parenting in America Today." *The Pew Research Center*. January 24, 2023. https://www.pewresearch.org/social-trends/2023/01/24/parenting-in-america-today.

Ziff, Lazar. *The Career of John Cotton: Puritanism and The American Experience*. Princeton: Princeton University Press, 1962.

2

In Thy Dark Streets
The Seminary Experience of Phillips Brooks

Robert D. Flanagan

When Phillips Brooks stepped off the steamer George Washington on to the pier at Alexandria, Virginia, he was as far from home as he had ever been.[1] He wrote later in the day that Alexandria was fifty years behind the times, meaning it felt like 1800.[2] He had left Boston and the northern non-slave states, entering an alien land.

After securing his trunk and arranging for its delivery, Phillips likely bought a newspaper. He was an avid reader after all. He hired a horse for uphill trip to the Virginia Theological Seminary (VTS), three miles to his west, and met one of the seminary's professors, Joseph Packard, at the Seminary gate.[3] Waiting for his horse to be saddled, his journey's last leg, which

---

1. The *Alexandria Gazette* advertised two steam ships traveling daily to Alexandria from Washington. They were the George Washington and the George Page. The Alice C. Price was being reconditioned and not available until April 8. Advertisements, *Alexandria Gazette*, November 7, 1856. See also Phillips Brooks to William G. Brooks, Jr. 7 Nov. 1856, Phillips Brooks Papers, bMS AM 1594.1, (39), folder 3, Houghton Library, Harvard University.

2. Phillips Brooks to William G. Brooks, Jr. November 7, 1856, bMS AM 1594.1, (39), folder 3.

3. Joseph Packard, "The Recollections of a Long Life," quoted in Allen, *Life and Letters*, 1:177.

had started in Boston on October 31, 1856, he likely read the November 7th morning edition of the *Alexandria Gazette*.

He was eager to learn of the 1856 US presidential election results.[4] Nothing was official. The paper gave the latest state electoral numbers and projected the outcome. The Southern Democratic candidate, James Buchanan would secure enough electoral college votes to defeat the Know Nothing party candidate and former US President, Millard Filmore and the Republican party's first presidential nominee, the US Senator from California and antislavery candidate, John C. Frémont. When the tally was compiled, the election had not been close. Frémont had even lost his home state and almost lost New York. Slavery would not be eliminated in the 1850s. Phillips would have read the article with disgust. He and his brothers were Frémont supporters.[5]

In the paper, he would have also read a pleasant article about the White Mountains and Franconia Notch, New Hampshire, describing its autumn splendor. The correspondent for the *Boston Evening Traveller* wrote about the tree colors: "In the White Mountains these effects are so wrought on a grandeur of scale, with nobler masses and more varied lights than anywhere else within our knowledge."[6] If Phillips continued reading, he would have read the "Running Slaves" article about four slaves seeking freedom on a ship that departed from Alexandria. The article concluded, "These Abolitionists thought it a good time, during the excitement of a political contest like the present, to abduct Southern property in the shape of slaves, without detection. They may find themselves mistaken."[7] Stories of slaves fleeing the South were not uncommon to Phillps. However, reading about its occurrence where he would reside for the next three years would have been unsettling.

If Phillips continued to read, perusing the classified advertisements, the alien land surrounding him would have become horrifyingly clear. Among the advertisements for black velvet ribbon, coffee, flour, and wool, a Joseph Bruin had placed an advertisement for Negroes, stating, "I wish to purchase any number of NEGROES, for which I will pay liberal prices.

4. "The Presidential Election," *Alexandria Gazette*, November 7, 1865, Friday morning edition.

5. Phillips Brooks to William G. Brooks, Jr. November 7, 1856, bMS AM 1594.1, (39), folder 3.

6. "The White Mountains," *Alexandria Gazette*, November 7, 1865, Friday morning edition.

7. "Running Slaves," *Alexandria Gazette*, November 7, 1865, Friday morning edition.

Those wishing to sell, will do well to call on me before selling, at my old stand at West End, Alexandria."[8] That same evening, Phillips' assessment of his new home was clear: "The South is a mean and a wretched country at best, so far as I have seen it. The line seems marked most plainly where the blessings cease and the curses begin, where men cease to own themselves and begin to own each other."[9] Virginia Theological Seminary was a long way from Harvard Yard.

Virginia Theological Seminary in the 1850s was very different from his Alma Mater in Cambridge. The Seminary was in the country, situated just outside the District of Columbia's southwestern edge amidst the farm country of northeast Virginia. From top floor of the campus' main building, Phillips would have seen Alexandria to his east and Washington was seven miles to the north with the reconstruction of the US Capitol Building's dome underway. The Seminary's approximately eighty acres of campus was a mixture of thick woods and fields. Students would cut and saw the wood needed for heating their rooms from the trees on campus. When their blades dulled, they would carry their saw with them as they walked to Alexandria and collect the Seminary's mail.[10]

Although Phillips did not appreciate the Seminary's facilities, the buildings and grounds had been recently improved. The institution built several buildings in the 1850s. The chapel was expanded and consecrated in 1855. St. George's Church (New York City) gave $4000, funding the building of St. George's Hall (1856).[11] A fireproof library building was complete in 1856 and the Maywood residence that year as well. Other pre-Civil War buildings include Bohlen and Meade Halls and the Wilderness.[12] A 1700s building named Oakwood was the southernmost of seven buildings

---

8. "Negroes Wanted," *Alexandria Gazette and Advertiser*, November 7, 1856.

9. Phillips Brooks to William G. Brooks, Jr. November 7, 1856, bMS AM 1594.1, (39), folder 3.

10. Cornelius Walker, *Sparrow*, 127–28.

11. St. George's Hall was listed on the Nov 1912 Fire Insurance map. (Library of Congress Maps Division, Washington D.C.), and located due west of the library. The building has since been demolished. The Addison Academic building sits on that location today. *Sanborn Fire Insurance Map from Alexandria, Independent Cities, Virginia.* Sanborn Map Company, Nov. 1912. Map. https://www.loc.gov/item/sanborn08968_006/.

12. The Wilderness has been thought to have been a brick residence located northwest of the current refectory. However, the early 1860 General Irvin McDowell and the Fire Insurance maps of 1902 and 1912 do not show the building. The maps call into question the building's precise location. It may have been a wooden structure, which did not last.

situated at the crest of the hill facing east.[13] When Phillips arrived at the Seminary, he would have entered the main gate to the east at the bottom of the hill.

The Seminary was at its eighteenth-century peak. The Seminary's Dean, Dr. Sparrow, noted, that the seminary, "appeared in May 1861 with its new buildings and its lush green grounds, resplendent with woods all around."[14] The student body had been growing steadily, and the class of 1856 included seventeen students from both Northern and Southern states. The approximate student body total was forty. Even so, compared to Harvard's gas-lit and coal heated buildings and its student body of three hundred, the Seminary would have seemed backwards, remote, and small.

From his first day forward, Phillips Brooks's Alexandria residency tried and tested him, challenging his preconceived notions and affirming his anti-slavery position. Witnessing the human suffering and cruelty of the slave-South changed him from an arrogant, sarcastic Bostonian Brahmin intellectual into a fledgling pastor who had empathy for others. His three-year seminary experience, however, was not atypical.

Philllips' seminary path is familiar to the many generations of American seminarians. His seminary decision came after a significant life change. Phillip closely held his choice of VTS, and some friends were dismayed at his career decision. He then struggled to adjust to his new surroundings at VTS. From the start, he was critical of his professors and classmates and desperately wanted to leave at the end of his first year.

His second year showed some maturation and spiritual growth. Phillips resolved to remain at VTS for another year but still had doubts. He blossomed academically, applying his Harvard-honed writing acumen. However, what truly separated Phillips from his classmates was his willingness to read widely despite the typical demanding second-year course load. He read voraciously from various subjects, including many non-religious texts, keeping detailed notebooks in which he commented on what he learned and further developed his thoughts.

Like seminarians across the two hundred years of seminary history, Phillips began transitioning to his new vocation in his final year at VTS. He started applying what he learned, giving sermons to his classmates and at

---

13. United States Army. Corps Of Engineers. *Detailed map of part of Virginia from Alexandria to the Potomac River above Washington, D.C. 186*. [186, 1860] Map. https://www.loc.gov/item/2001627680/.

14. Booty, *Mission and Ministry*, 111.

Sharon Chapel. He tried out and exercised his new priestly and preaching identities. The faculty also offered him a chance to redeem his prior teaching failure, asking him to instruct the Preparatory Department's students. Phillips fielded employment inquiries from several churches as well. Like many seminarians, he found his final seminary days filled with opportunities to apply his learning and foster his budding ministry. Both were tempered by angst about his competency and worthiness to become a priest.

1855–SUMMER 1857

After his Harvard graduation in the spring of 1855, the nineteen-year-old Phillips Brooks began a teaching career at his alma mater, the Boston Latin School. Founded in 1635, the school is the oldest school in America and one of its most prestigious public schools, educating many of Boston's brightest young people. As the great-grandson of the Honorable Samuel Phillips Jr., who founded the Phillips Academy Andover, and nephew of John and Elizabeth Phillips, the co-founders of the Phillips Exter Academy, teaching was an easy choice and seemed a natural calling for Phillips. He was, however, barely a man when he started as a school usher or teacher. The academic year began well for Phillips, teaching a class of boys, but three months into the semester, the headmaster assigned him to a class of thirty-five teenagers, ages fifteen to seventeen.

Phillips' new class had been unruly. Two previous instructors had fled, and without the necessary classroom management experience and skills to lead such a group, he foundered. The classroom chaos continued and even escalated under Phillips' watch. His relationship with the teenagers unraveled quickly. On December 9, 1855, he wrote his friend George "Top" C. Sawyer, also a young teacher himself at the Phillips Exeter Academy, lamenting his new situation: "They are the most disagreeable set of creatures without exception that I ever met with."[15] The new year did not improve the classroom situation. In a January 19, 1856 letter to Top, Phillips exhorted, "I believe they consider me just now as a sort of dragon with his claws cut, a gigantic ogre who would like to eat them, but hasn't the stomach to do it."[16] Top apparently gave Phillips a new strategy, but the situation had already

---

15. Phillps Brooks to George C. Sawyer, 9 Dec. 1855, quoted in Allen, *Life and Letters*, 1:115.

16. Phillps Brooks to George C. Sawyer, 19 Jan. 1855, quoted in Allen, *Life and Letters*, 1:115.

become toxic. Phillips added, "It may be needful to explain that I have changed my class. The one I had before were splendid little fellows; these are tough old sinners with iniquity of some sixteen springs, summers, autumns, and winters on their grim hoary heads."[17] By early February, he quit.

Phillips struggled with failing so publicly in his family's occupation. Like any young person at the beginning of their working years and having stumbled in his first job, Phillips was introspective and, as a man of his times, melodramatic. By late summer, however, his mood had changed; he still had hope. Writing privately on the evening of August 14, 1856, "If I am to choose a life for *myself*, which I am to live and for which I am to answer, let the choice be *really mine*, let me say to my advisors: I receive your advice but no dictation."[18] He admitted his failure but holds to hope for himself, continuing, "I have failed myself most signally in teaching school, but I am not yet quite ready to acknowledge myself wholly unequal to all this wide world's work."

After private conversations with his mother, father, and family priest, Dr. Vinton, Phillips chose to study for the ministry at the Seminary of the Protestant Episcopal Church in Virginia.[19] In the fall, Phillips traveled to Alexandria, dawdling through several cities, visiting friends, and arriving in November after the semester's commencement. As such, he was the last student to arrive and got the seminary's worst room. Phillips described it in a letter to his brother William on November 7, 1856: "My lordly apartment is a garret in an old building called the Wilderness. Its furniture at present consists of a bedstead and a washstand. I looked in for a moment, threw down my carpet bag and ran. I suppose I have to sleep there to-night, but I'm sure I don't know how."[20] His sparse accommodations and the room's low ceiling disappointed the six-foot-four Bostonian.

His housing inconvenience paled in respect to his first encounter with slavery. The 1790 Massachusetts census listed no enslaved people in the Commonwealth.[21] Slavery had effectively and legally ended in Massachusetts more than three decades before Phillips' birth in 1835. Phillips hoped

17. Phillips Brooks to George C. Sawyer, 19 Jan. 1855, quoted in Allen, *Phillips Brooks*, 20.

18. Allen, *Phillips Brooks*, 33.

19. Allen, *Life and Letters*, 142.

20. Phillips Brooks to William G. Brooks, Jr., 7 Nov. 1856, bMS AM 1594.1, (39), folder 3.

21. The Massachusetts Court System. "Massachusetts Constitution and the Abolition of Slavery." https://www.mass.gov/guides/massachusetts-constitution-and-the-abolition-of-slavery.

the newly formed Republican party's presidential candidate and opponent of slavery, John Charles Frémont, would win the 1856 election and was duly disappointed by James Buchanan's presidential victory. Extolling to William in his November 7th letter, "I am a stronger Frémont man than ever, since seeing Buchanan and Fillmore States, and know nothing that I would not do to change the results."[22]

Thus, the slave-South shocked the twenty-year-old. Phillips explained his reaction to Top on November 14, 1856: "But the people are wretched, shiftless, uninteresting, lazy, deceitful. I suppose it is one of the best places to see the sad effects of slavery on the white population, degrading and unmanning them."[23] With his prejudice evident, he also wrote of an initial encounter with enslaved people, "I met a long caravan of wagons coming from the interior of the state manned by slaves which gave me more of an idea of my own impression of slave life than anything I have seen yet. The darkies seem jolly and happy, which, to my mind, makes it all the worse."[24]

For any seminarian, the early seminary experience is a mixture of an introduction to graduate-level academic learning and forming social connections, paving the path to spiritual formation. It is a process of unlearning preconceptions about ordained life and adapting to a new environment after leaving one's cherished home. Phillips went through this process just like any other seminarian.

The transition to seminary is often formidable. The bright, shiny days of departure from home and the anticipation of a new experience where one may encounter God anew can give way to regret, remorse, fear, and resignation. Like salt melting on a blade in a forge, indicating the time for quenching and hardening in cold oil, the seminarian begins the rigors of academic study and community integration and assimilation, often with a sudden shock. While Phillips efficiently handled the academic demands, he strained to make friends and fully engage with seminary life. On November 14, 1856, he explained to Top, "I live almost entirely by myself, see little or nothing of other students, who seem to be an extremely good but not particularly interesting set of young men. I imagine they don't think much of me." On November 28, 1856, he wrote to his brother William about a class

22. Phillips Brooks to William G. Brooks, Jr., 7 Nov. 1856, bMS AM 1594.1, (39), folder 3.

23. Phillps Brooks to Willliam C. Sawyer, 14 Nov. 1856, quoted in Allen, *Phillips Brooks*, 40.

24. Phillps Brooks to Willliam C. Sawyer, 14 Nov. 1856, quoted in Allen, *Phillips Brooks*, 40–41.

party he attended: "There were twelve students and three ladies, the latter being apparently rather a scarce article in these parts. We stayed from 7:30 to twelve, and altogether it was not remarkably pleasant."[25]

The slave issue contributed to Phillips's hardship. The seminary's student body came from the North and South. Phillips's class included Virginia, Delaware, New York, and Pennsylvania students, among other states. In a December 18, 1856 letter to his father, Phillips explained that Southern students railed against Northern students who had been meeting with the enslaved servants of the seminary, even preaching to them.[26] He wrote, "Another [seminarian], who has preached some in the neighborhood has been informed that there was tar and feathers ready for him if he went far from the seminary."[27] Another seminarian explained, "The 'dear old seminary' was not a very comfortable place then for anti-slavery men, such as a few of us were, especially if we exercised and claimed the right of free speech. When one of our fellow students was notified that he would be 'tarred and feathered' if he did not leave, Phillips stood nobly by him, and declared that the men of the North must all leave together and publicly declare their reason for withdrawing."[28] Even at the secluded Alexandria seminary campus, the nation's boiling troubles seeped into daily community life.

Phillips was against slavery but was not above prejudice. In a December 23, 1857 letter to his brother George, Phillips explained a blatant dehumanizing account. He told an elderly slave to stand on his head while he—Brooks—placed two nickels on the edge of his desk. The man did as he was bidden but then quickly righted himself, grabbed the money, and bolted off without a word. Brooks commented that the slave seemed ungrateful.[29] The encounter with the slave highlights Phillips' blind spots of classism and racial prejudice.

By the spring of 1857, Phillips concluded he was finished with the seminary. On March 16, 1857, he wrote his father, stating, "I really begin to have serious doubts whether it will be worthwhile for me to come back here for two more years."[30] Time did not change his attitude. Writing his

---

25. Phillips Brooks to William G. Brooks, 28 Nov. 1856, bMS AM 1594.1 (3) folder.

26. Phillips Brooks to William G. Brooks, Sr., 18 Dec. 1856, bMS AM 1594.1 (3) folder.

27. Phillips Brooks to William G. Brooks, Sr., 18 Dec. 1856, bMS AM 1594.1 (3) folder.

28. Allen, *The Life and Letters*, 1:158.

29. Phillips Brooks to George Brooks, 23 Dec. 1857, bMS AM 2022, (26). See also John F. Woolverton, *Education of Phillips Brooks*, 67.

30. Phillips Brooks to William G. Brooks, Sr., 23 Dec. 1857, bMS AM 1594.1 (4) folder.

father on May 8th, he announced, "I really can't help feeling every day as I told you a good while ago that this seminary is not what it ought to be or what I want."[31] He was disappointed with the teaching style, likely different from Harvard's, and felt that his peers lacked appropriate scholarly training. His vexation toward the faculty was particularly harsh: "The faculty is only second rate I consider (There is no use of mincing it—egregiously dull and stupid)."[32] He pointedly criticized one professor, saying that while he respected him as a good man and a good Christian, "as a scholar and professor is inferior (has outlived his usefulness years ago)." Phillips concluded, "I may say too that the ablest young men here are seriously thinking of leaving this summer."[33]

Phillips pursued transferring seminaries. He and another student wrote to Andover Theological Seminary—Phillips' family seminary. At some point in June, they received a reply rejecting their inquiry. In his June 21, 1857 letter to his father, Phillips explained that it was "a very short and very stuffy and to my idea very ungentlemanly note" in which Dr. Park of Andover "didn't encourage our going to Andover at all."[34] Phillips flirted with attending a seminary just forming in Philadelphia as well, but, for an unknown reason, he did not seriously consider it. In August 1957, Phillips visited the Berkeley Divinity School, which had been Trinity College's (Hartford, Connecticut) theology department, but in 1854, moved to Middletown, CT. (The seminary eventually moved to New Haven to affiliate with Yale Divinity School.) Phillips did not like it and returned to Virginia for another year, but not without complaint. In October 1857, he grumbled a final time: "You can hardly imagine how disagreeable it is to be back among Southern men after New England."[35]

Phillips' first-year seminary experience was not unusual. Seminarians often complain about their professors, classmates, accommodations, and food. While teaching the Introduction to Priestly Ministry course, I fielded complaints from several students. One found life particularly difficult, stating that the campus lacked any community. While I agreed that the community life of that particular seminary was sparse, what she desired would not likely be found at another seminary. Like Phillips, she explored

---

31. Phillips Brooks to William G. Brooks, Sr., 8 May 1857, bMS AM 1594.1 (4) folder.
32. Phillips struck through "stupid," but it was still readable.
33. Phillips Brooks to William G. Brooks, Sr., 8 May 1857, bMS AM 1594.1 (4) folder.
34. Phillips Brooks to William G. Brooks, Sr., 21 June 1857, bMS AM 1594.1 (4) folder.
35. Phillips Brooks to William G. Brooks, Sr., Aug. 1857, bMS, AM 1594.1 (4) folder.

other institutions, but unlike him, she switched. Often seminarian angst and dissatisfaction are due to spiritual formation, changing from what one believes seminary and the priesthood should be to seeing them for exactly what they are. The seminarian experience involves God's shaping, at times like steel on an anvil, a person into a better self and better ready to handle the highly stressful work of pastoring people in distress.

Phillips needed to soften his youthful sarcasm and quick criticism that often bordered on harshness. He was a Harvard man and a Boston Brahmin. Gillis J. Harp explains, "Phillips Brooks was born into a society led by a socially conservative old-money elite that had a strong sense of *noblesse oblige*."[36] He was well-educated and situated in the echelon of Boston's high society. To become a great preacher and leader of the nineteenth-century Episcopal Church, he had to soften his educational snobbery and loosen his buttoned-up Boston way. His second year in isolation at the seminary overlooking the nation's capital would assist him in the former.

FALL 1857–SUMMER 1858

While Phillips Brooks may have complained about many aspects of seminary, he kept his academic discipline. From the outset, he kept notebooks, which included reading notations, his musings about life and future ministry, and verses and poems. Of the latter, the following poem summaries his thoughts regarding his studies,

> How vain is our knowing unless we can feel.
> How little mere study alone can reveal.
> How the slow waves of learning creep page after page,
> Like the wearing of torrents, an inch in an age.[37]

Much of his studies came quickly, and one did not. In a letter to Top, he described Hebrew as "the queerest old language I ever saw."[38] And yet Phillips persisted.

By the spring of 1857, Phillips understood that he must change his perspective and sheltered high-society viewpoint. He realized he needed to comprehend the human condition with its elations and sufferings to reach people. In his notebook, he wrote,

---

36. Harp, *Brahmin Prophet*, 11.
37. Allen, *Life and Letters*, 1:186.
38. Letter to G.C. Sawyer, November 14, 1856.

> Until we have learned the universal language of human sympathy, how can we hope to speak so that all may hear us, and be drawn to us by what they hear? While we speak thus, each in the selfish tongue of our own interest or passions, our words will come sealed to the ears of our fellows, and all the consciousness that we are heard and understood by others, or the sweeter feeling that the world is better for our words, will all be lost.[39]

Phillips recognized that one's perspective could be a stumbling block to a deep connection with others. A person's worldview could limit what people hear. For him, the responsibility lay on the speaker—the preacher—to learn how to be sympathetic. The way Phillips chose to learn the language of sympathy separated him from all but a few seminarians across the age.

Phillips read to unearth the human condition. His second-year academic workload was full. He studied the Hebrew and Christian scriptures in their original language, Ecclesiastical History, and Systematic Theology.[40] For most students, those four subjects would completely occupy their day, not so for Phillips. Alexander V.G. Allen provides an unabridged list of Phillips readings.[41] He read no less than eleven Greek writers, including Plato's *Phaedo* and Plutarch's *De Oraculorum Defectu*. The six early church fathers he read included Origen, Philo, and Chrysostom. His classic philosophical study comprised sixteen texts. Allen also notes that Phillips read Horace, Seneca, Tacitus, Lactantius, Ambrose, and Jerome. The twenty-nine English authors included Bacon, Coleridge, Keats, Chaucer, Shakespeare, Matthew Arnold, and George Herbert. Phillips also read another fifteen assorted texts, including Alexander Pope's *Eloisa to Abelard*, Izaak Walton's *The Compleat Angler*, Henry Ward Beecher's *Life Thoughts*, and Frederick William Faber's *Growth in Holiness*. He found Goethe's work intriguing as well. Allen's list ends with several French works. Phillips read nearly one hundred additional books and essays during this period.

His urge to study came from his soul. He recognized that his elite upbringing and education left him short. He was determined to correct that gap. He wrote, "If Nature is twenty years building our bodies, let us grudge no needful time to build our mind . . . let us shrink from no length of labor, or minuteness of finish, or conscientious thoroughness of every part of every

---

39. Allen, *Life and Letters*, 1:195.
40. Allen, *Letters and Life*, 1:217.
41. Allen, *Letters and Life*, 1:218–19.

work that is entrusted to our hands."[42] What he sought to build in himself took time to develop. He attempted to strip away the lacquer of cultural refinement.

At its core, Phillips Brooks's quest was not to discover truth but the Christian faith. He needed to explore the writings of others to realize life's meaning and faith's source. He had to move from his enlightened secular educational perspective to serving of God. He wrote,

> We overlook too much the common daily blessings that religion brings. Not least among these is the faculty of finding joy in little things, recognizing their divine bestowal, finding still higher blessedness in living out our gratitude to God.[43]

His observations of nature and human life pointed him toward God. As his examination of non-religious texts continued, he found the answers in his religious and theological studies. He summarized the contrast as such,

> I take up Homer, and the years are singing round me, and the truths of Troy-time, grown truer ever since, are linking me to human nature and divine. I read La Place, and Nature's riddle grows no less a mystery, but more a thing of fellowship with mind, and God who made it ... I open my New Testament, and native purity and truth melt in the holiness of Jesus' life. What I sought I found. I grow the safer as I grow wiser now. Safety and wisdom fade away in love. "I am the resurrection and the life."[44]

The immense amount of reading led him back to the New Testament, the Gospels, and Jesus. His quest ended with a deeper faith and stronger religious fealty. He also honed his thinking to speak faith to people of all stripes.

For many seminarians, the second year flashes by. They have figured out the academic pattern, knowing better the semester's peaks and valleys when assignments pile up and the tension mounts. Second-year student anxiety is lower because they have found at least a couple of friends, know what to expect during worship and prayer services, and have a favorite seat in the classroom and a decent residential room. Life may still be challenging, but students have a handle on the demands. By the middle of the

---

42. Allen, *Letters and Life*, 1:236.
43. Allen, *Life and Letters*, 1:253.
44. Allen, *Life and Letters*, 1:260.

second year, students know they are halfway and can glimpse a glint of their future profession's glow.

1858–1859

Phillips Brooks moved from theory to practice in his final year at VTS. He began to apply his voluminous reading and notes to his sermon writing. He preached in class and at a congregation near the seminary, and the faculty asked him to teach in the Preparatory Department, a program that helped priest candidates with weak academic skills prepare themselves for the three-year graduate degree program. He also accepted his first ministry position.

Unlike contemporary seminarians who often begin preaching before seminary or during their first year, Phillips only preached in his final academic year. His first efforts did not go well. The great Episcopal Church preacher was not a natural. Like many seminarians before and after him, preaching was a skill he had to learn. In a November 6, 1958 letter to William, he wrote,

> Some how the work I am at begins to look very different and strange to me. Do you know I feel as I never felt before, to find myself here within eight months of the ministry? Whether it is getting at sermon-writing that makes me feel more than ever how weak I am to go about the world's greatest work, I certainly do feel it fearfully to-night.[45]

Phillips recognized the importance of preaching the Good News and its centrality to the clergy's work. He also trembled at his ability to complete it successfully.

Brooks preached at Sharon Chapel,[46] which was founded in 1848 and located three miles west of the seminary across a small valley. In the fall of 2000, I attended a Sunday service and was surprised to discover the congregation remembered its long-ago seminarian, Phillips Brooks. The parish even named an exterior door after him, oddly located in the sanctuary's chancel area. I returned to the church in 2023 to inquire about the Phillips Brooks door. Even though the sanctuary space had changed, been

---

45. Phillips Brooks to William G. Brooks, Jr., 6 Nov. 1858, quoted in Allen, *Phillips Brooks*, 87.

46. Sharon Chapel is now All Saints Sharon Chapel and is still located on its original property on Franconia Road, Alexandria.

renovated, and moved in the subsequent one-hundred-seventy-plus years, Phillips' door is an architectural fixture.

To peel away the layers of history, I interviewed several long-time parishioners on November 5, 2023. After the 10:30 Sunday service, Jane Delbridge, Donna Smith, and Joyce Goins sat with me in the white-walled parish hall and delightfully explained the events of Phillips Brooks's first sermon. Their account matched the one I had heard twenty years before.

The sanctuary had been a simple structure with a lectern near the altar area. Phillips began his sermon, speaking rapidly with shallow breaths and short pauses. Phillips finished quickly. He looked out over the nave, anticipating the congregation's positive reaction. None came. His nerves overcame him. Phillips then turned to the nearest window, climbed through it, and ran back to the seminary.

In his biography, Alexander Allen acknowledges that Phillips's first sermon at Sharon Chapel did not succeed. He confirmed the Delbridge, Smith, and Goins's historical account, adding one crucial detail: "There is a tradition that Phillips Brooks was not successful in these ventures; indeed he is said to have made a total failure on his first attempt, receiving as his only encouragement the advice to try it again."[47] Allen's account aligns with All Saints Sharon Chapel members' oral history, providing confidence in the story's veracity. Phillips' first attempt at preaching was inauspicious.

Phillips's letters home were silent about the embarrassing occasion. In his November 6th letter to William, he only stated that his first sermons were "poor." He added, "I do enjoy the work, and with all my unfitness for it, look forward to a happy life in trying to do it."[48] In a later essay titled "On the Pulpit and Popular Skepticism," Phillips recalled his first sermon. Although he does not mention if he gave it at Sharon Chapel, the Seminary chapel, or in a class, his thoughts conveyed his modest preaching start. He wrote, "I am sure that the sermon never was preached again. Its lack of simplicity and lack of Christ no doubt belonged together. It was probably an attempt to define doctrine instead of to show a man, a God, a Saviour."[49] He also shared his thoughts with his brother Frederick: "You know I was never much of a speaker."[50]

---

47. Allen, *Life and Letters*, 290.

48. Phillips Brooks to William G. Brooks, Jr., 6 Nov. 1858, quoted in Allen, *Phillips Brooks*, 87.

49. Phillips Brooks, "On the Pulpit and Popular Skepticism," 74.

50. Allen, *Life and Letters*, 290.

Phillips was committed to the task, however. Despite his uninspiring first attempt, he remained at Sharon Chapel and seemed to improve. Phillips explained to William his ministry at Sharon Chapel:

> I have undertaken this year to preach plain sermons to a small congregation of from fifty to seventy-five people at one of the stations near the seminary, and feel that I am better for the work, more and deeper sympathy with simple, honest men, and a clearer light into what common men's minds are doing, and how they may be taught to do better and nobler things.[51]

Phillips may have crafted and delivered poor messages initially but did not quit. The experience humbled and forced him to reexamine himself. Although challenging to receive, Phillips' listeners gave him vital feedback, which he maturely took. He did not blame the "common man" for a lack of understanding but himself, the preacher, who needed to communicate better.

Phillips changed his approach. He preached extemporaneously to the Sharon Chapel congregation. He wrote Frederick about it: "Lately I have been cultivating the extempore address, and, though no orator as Brutus is, it goes pretty glib. I expect to preach so a good deal."[52] While Phillps felt comfortable preaching without a text at Sharon Chapel, he often preached using entirely hand-written, complete texts after leaving the seminary.

Phillips also received a measure of redemption during his final seminary year. Soon after returning to campus that fall, Dr. Sparrow informed Phillips that he would like him to "take charge of the preparatory school." Within a week, the faculty had offered him the position, and Phillips began to teach Latin and Greek to a class of thirteen, preparing for seminary. Dr. Sparrow had even indicated a permanent faculty position would be available if he stayed on after graduation.[53] Phillips seemed to enjoy overseeing these adult students. He wrote his father on November 16, 1858, stating, "The school comes on well, takes a good deal of time, but is not unpleasant work."[54] However, like most seminarians, the pull of the pulpit was too strong. Phillips was not destined for a professorship.

---

51. Phillips Brooks to William G. Brooks, Jr., 6 Nov. 1858, quoted in Allen, *Phillips Brooks*, 88.

52. Allen, *Life and Letters*, 290–91.

53. Allen, *Life and Letters*, 275.

54. Phillips Brooks to William G. Brooks, Sr., 16 Nov. 1858, bMS AM 1594.1 (5) folder.

In Thy Dark Streets

The spring of 1859 solidified Brooks's track. On Sunday, March 6, 1859, he received an offer to lead a parish. He wrote his parents about the event the following day: "You can imagine my surprise yesterday on being waited upon by two gentlemen who evidently came on business. They were a committee of the vestry of the Church of the Advent in Philadelphia and came to bring me a call to become their rector in July."[55] Phillips had fielded an inquiry from a San Francisco church, which he did not pursue, and his mentor, Dr. Vinton, who was now leading a church in Philadelphia, had wanted Phillips to be his assistant. So, Phillips had choices for employment.

Phillips wanted the Advent position but had two worries. He wrote his brother, William, saying, "So here I am all adrift." He did not want to offend Dr. Vinton. He continued, "I must choose now between Dr. V.'s assistantship and the Advent, and if I choose Advent then good-by to all the Doctor's friendliness in future."[56] His other concern was the Bishop of Massachusetts, Manton Eastburn, who, like most bishops, wanted Phillips to return to his diocese to work.

The latter concern was quickly resolved. The bishop replied to Phillips, giving him his consent. On March 10, 1859, he wrote,

> I had been counting with pleasant anticipation upon your services, during your term of deacon's orders at least... But if you are persuaded that you hear the voice of God in this application, calling you to that particular field of labor, I should of course shrink from interposing any obstacle and I cheerfully give my consent.[57]

With his bishop's approval, Phillips accepted the position but still worried about his relationship with Dr. Vinton, who did not immediately write Phillips a response. It was not until the fall, after Phillips had preached several evening sermons at the Church of the Holy Trinity, Philadelphia, Dr. Vinton's parish, and Dr. Vinton had preached at the Advent's Sunday evening, that the two reconciled fully.[58]

Phillips Brooks's final year was typical for a seminarian. He moved from theory to practice, applying what he had learned the previous two

---

55. Phillips Brooks to William G. Brooks, Sr., and Mary Anne Phillips Brooks, 6 Mar. 1859, bMS AM 1594.1 (6) folder.

56. Allen, *Life and Letters*, 294.

57. Bishop Eastburn to Phillips Brooks, 10 Mar. 1859, quoted in Allen, *Life and Letters*, 294.

58. Allen, *Life and Letter*, 336.

years. He was a novice preacher who became better as the year went on. Phillips tried different preaching styles, which helped him become confident about his future vocation. He also found meaning and purpose in his final seminary year. Like many, Phillps rose to seminary leadership, teaching in the Preparatory Department and using his academic skills to help others pursue ordained ministry. He had to navigate his transition, as well. Phillips asked his bishop to be released, which, like many seminarians, he found anxiety-producing. Bishops hold much power over priest candidates; many use that power to fill positions within their diocese. Phillips left the seminary prepared for ministry but not fully formed as the priest and preacher he would become.

CONCLUSION

Phillips Brooks's Virginia years dramatically changed him. He was a Boston Brahmin, a member of the Phillips line from his mother's side. Leaving Boston for the 1850s South shaped his worldview and humbled him. It opened him to the breadth of humanity and gave him a lived experience from which he could draw empathy for the plight of others. His seminary time was not an Abrahamic experience but a John-the-Baptist one. Phillips left the comforts of home and the halls of prestige for a desolate place under siege by the ravages of slavery. In the wilderness, he developed his faith and hope in Christ, which allowed him to begin his ministry. He was a young man full of potential with a message of Christ befitting the time.

Phillips' decision to remain at VTS was for the best. He reviled much of mid-nineteenth-century Southern culture, and his time there gave him perspective. Had he attended the Congregationalist Andover Seminary, he would have been unfamiliar with the Episcopal tradition and struggled as an Episcopal priest. VTS was an Episcopal seminary, even with its Evangelical leanings. At the Northern Episcopal seminaries, Phillips would not have experienced the Southern culture in all its depravity. The northern institutions were not fully anti-slavery or abolitionist but existed in a world Phillips knew. What Phillips saw and lived strengthened his resolve and grounded him in Christian hope.

His isolation gave him time and focus. Phillips read. If VTS had an urban locale, Phillips could have found other distractions. He could have visited friends in New York City or traveled back to Boston. But his time in desolate Virginia and Buchanan's pro-slavery government across the

Potomac River kept him on campus and reading. Phillips filled in his academic gaps and let his curiosity drive him to understand the human experience. He wanted to know what made people think and act as they did. Phillips desired to discover the essence of humanity. His time and focus allowed him to cultivate and improve his preaching skills. Phillips would have to refine his pastoral care skills after he graduated, but his ability to preach would give him the time to become a pastor.

Phillips Brooks's seminary experience gave him what he needed to be a competent priest and preacher. He gained humility and insight. He discovered empathy and a desire to care for others. Phillips suffered through adversity and gained patience while at VTS. He adequately learned the skills of his vocation. Like John the Baptist, Phillps returned to proclaim the good news of Jesus in a country about to erupt into civil war.

BIBLIOGRAPHY

Allen, Alexander V. G. *Life and Letters of Phillips Brooks.* 2 vols. New York: Dutton, 1900.

———. *Phillips Brooks (1835–1893): Memories of His Life with Extracts from His Letters and Note-Books.* New York: Dutton, 1907.

Booty, John. *Mission and Ministry: A History of the Virginia Theological Seminary.* Harrisburg, PA: Morehouse, 1995.

Brooks, Phillips. "On the Pulpit and Popular Skepticism." In *Essays and Addresses.* Princeton: Princeton Review, 1879.

Harp, Gillis J. *Brahmin Prophet: Phillips Brooks and the Path of Liberal Protestantism.* Lanham, MD: Rowman & Littlefield, 2003.

Packard, Joseph. "The Recollections of a Long Life." *Protestant Episcopal Review* (April 1897).

Walker, Cornelius. *The Life and Correspondence of Rev. William Sparrow, D.D.* Philadelphia: Jaems Hammond, 1876.

Woolverton, John F. *The Education of Phillips Brooks.* Urbana: University of Illinois Press, 1995.

3

Where Faith Holds Wide the Door
Phillips Brooks in Philadelphia

Rachel Wenner Gardner

I walk past a large portrait of Phillips Brooks every day on the way to my office. He is placed next to the architectural rendering of the original church plans, which includes a large spire—a spire, which Phillips Brooks fought against and was successful in defeating in favor of a square bell tower. Every time I give someone a tour of the place, I joke that Phillips Brooks lives in perpetuity next to the thing he hated the most. In many ways, this was his experience in Philadelphia—ultimately successful, but not without battle scars and stretch marks. In Philadelphia, away from his family and on his own in this new vocation, he had the freedom to explore and grow. Brooks was thrust into celebrity and popularity at a young age as well and experienced tragedy, heartbreak, and disappointment, and he discovered the real nitty—gritty of being a priest and leading a church.

Of all my predecessors, in the parishes I have worked, I understand, admire, and resonate with Brooks the most. His values, principles, and sense of duty drove him. Despite the ways the church frustrated him, blocked his dreams, and broke his heart, he remained dedicated to her. He found joy in the people around him, and was a fiercely devoted son, brother, uncle, and friend. Brooks also deeply loved and respected children, never talking down to them, but treating them as equal spiritual beings who need God's love as much as anyone. He seldom let fear get in the way of doing what is right and spoke the truth, even when it might have cost him. Some of my predecessors have felt Brooks's shadow looming over them at The Church of the Holy Trinity, but I never have. Instead, I feel proud to follow in his footsteps and grateful for his wisdom, guidance, and presence as his spirit walks beside me. Brooks's heart and spirit pulse through this church as we, too, extend our doors and our hearts wide open to our neighbors and neighborhood.

MOVING TO PHILADELPHIA

Phillips Brooks could have taken several different paths after leaving seminary. Many including his family, expected him to begin his career at a church in Boston, but Philadelphia called to him. In time, he will become known as a shining star—for his eloquent speaking and powerful sermons, for his conviction that every person deserves dignity and empowerment, for his devotion to the church and love of children. People could see this about Brooks early on in his life and work. Some wondered why he would take a small church in Philadelphia, rather than begin his rise to fame at a more prestigious place. But those who knew Brooks knew that his sense of duty vastly outweighed his sense of celebrity. He was a deeply humble man—even at the height of his career—who never sought fame nor thought of himself worthy of any of the praise or acclaim so often heaped on him.

His childhood rector, Rev. Dr. Alexander Vinton, had just taken a position at a new church in Philadelphia. Dr. Vinton invited him to work at The Church of the Holy Trinity, which was fast becoming a prominent church in the burgeoning neighborhood of Rittenhouse Square. Brooks declined, telling his brother, William, "You know, and I know, that Dr. Vinton's Holy Trinity would be a place of far more prominence and promise of future eminence and brilliant calls, but I am going to this church . . . they are kind and simple people, and ready and anxious to make their minister's life a pleasant one."[1] Thus, following his graduation from seminary, and despite everything that might draw him elsewhere, Brooks came to Philadelphia and settled at the Church of the Advent.

In a letter to his brother, William, Brooks explained his choice. "One thing I am sure of—(the position at Advent) was not accepted from any ambitious desire of occupying a conspicuous place. I am going, as I believe,

---

1. Letter from Brooks to his brother, William, dated March 17, 1859, Allen, *Life and Letters*, 296.

in a sincere feeling that I *ought* to go, in an earnest conviction that there is work to be done, and that by a strength above my own I shall be helped to do it."[2]

On July 10, 1859, Brooks presided over his first service at the Church of the Advent. The *Philadelphia Press* covered this event, describing Brooks as "a young gentlemen of fine attainments . . . (whose) reading of the morning lessons was not without marks of modesty and distrust of self . . . yet his manner on the whole was graceful and quite indicative of adaptation to the solemn office to which he had been called."[3]

While Brooks loved his work with the congregation, and often spoke of enjoying the people with whom he worked, he also found leading the church a lonely task. Writing to William again, he described his work as "tolerable lonesome work . . . I wish I had somebody just to speak two words to . . . that wouldn't look . . . quite so much as if they were talking to the minister."[4] And despite a growing congregation (often drawing the ire of his colleagues who said he was taking away their parishioners) and a widening reputation as an excellent preacher, he often doubted whether or not he was effective as a priest in that church. He complained to his family in letters of being "fearfully tired" from the unrelenting pace of the congregation.[5] He preached two sermons each week, held a Sunday evening lecture and Wednesday evening Bible study, taught children's Sunday school on Wednesday afternoons, visited members in his off time, all while doing the administrative work of clergy in charge of a parish. After two years, he remarked that the congregation had grown so large they were "mostly strangers," which added to his loneliness. He remarked that he was troubled with "blue spots," longing to be home in Boston with his family. To his father, he wrote, "I have been thinking lately that if I made any change, it would be probably for a smaller and not a larger field. Advent looks all bright, but there are some discouraging things about it."[6]

As word of Phillips Brooks's success spread far and fast, larger, and more prominent churches in Boston, San Francisco, New York, Cincinnati, Cleveland, Harrisburg, Providence, Newport, and other churches

---

2. Letter from Brooks to William, dated March 17, 1859, Allen, *Life and Letters* 1:295–296.

3. *Philadelphia Press* July 11, 1859, Allen, *Life and Letters*, 1:330.

4. Letter from Brooks to William, dated July 16, 1859, Allen, *Life and Letters*, 1:332.

5. Letter from Brooks to his father, dated August 6, 1859, Allen, *Life and Letters*, 1:354.

6. Letter from Brooks to William, dated February 1861 Allen, *Life and Letters*, 1:363.

in Philadelphia tried in vain to entice him away from the Church of the Advent. Because of his duty to and sense of need from Advent, he was not swayed to leave. Yet, with each new recruitment attempt, the whisper in the back of his mind grew slightly louder: *should I be doing something more?*

The country around Brooks was rumbling with news of an impending Civil War. He rejoiced at Lincoln's election as President of the United States, saying to William in February of 1861, "I saw 'Abe' . . . I believe he will do the work. At any rate, it's a satisfaction to have an honest man there." As the War began in spring of 1861, he was swept up in the excitement of doing something for the good of the country. Writing to his father, "Isn't it great to see people in our degenerate days willing to go to work for a principle as our people are doing now? Our lecture room at Advent has been a tailor's shop for the last week, with the ladies making clothes for the volunteers."[7]

Amid all of this, Holy Trinity began intensively courting Brooks to be their second Rector. Dr. Vinton had accepted a call in New York and had recommended Brooks as his heir apparent. Throughout Brooks's three years at Advent, Holy Trinity asked him to become their rector no fewer than six times. Repeatedly, Brooks turned down the offers.

Brooks was not interested in notoriety or fame. He was raised and encouraged by his parents to "let no human praise make (him) proud, but be humble as the Master (he) serves."[8] He was not impressed by or inspired to be more. "The world (is) ruled and managed so often by its little and its greater men."[9] In spite of the opportunity and pressure from the wider church, Brooks held firm in his ministry at Advent. "Beginning to allow ourselves insincere pretentions of belief is like the beginning to take opium . . . pleasant and soothing at first . . . But you have to increase your dose every day."[10] He was reading Mason's *Said of Milton* at the time and wrote down this quote in his journals:

> As a Christian, humiliation before God was a duty the meaning of which he knew full well; but as a man moving among other men, he possessed in that moral seriousness the stoic scorn of temptation which characterized him a spring of ever present pride, dignifying his whole bearing among his fellows and at times arousing him to a kingly intolerance. (*Said of Milton*, Mason, I:237).

---

7. Allen, *Life and Letters*, 1:367.
8. Letter to Brooks from his mother, dated April 3, 1860, Allen, *Life and Letters*, 1:347.
9. Journal entry by Brooks, dated 1860. Allen, *Life and Letters*, 1:350.
10. Allen, *Life and Letters*, 1:357.

In March of 1861, Dr. Vinton preached his last sermon as Rector of Holy Trinity. Immediately following the service, the church voted to invite Brooks as Rector. In a letter to his brother, William, he wrote "They gave a call last Tuesday evening, backing it with a six-page letter from the congregation full of reasons why I could come."[11] Brooks was flattered and tempted, but he did not go. "I have concluded not to go, and have signified as much to Dr. Vinton . . . I don't see how I can properly leave Advent now"[12] as the church had taken out a sizeable loan, and he felt obligated to help them pay it off before he could leave.

For six months, Holy Trinity continued to court and call Brooks to be their rector. Brooks acquiesced to interview with them, but he turned down the position. Then, in November 1861, Brooks wrote to his parents, "I have resigned the Advent today and shall accept The Holy Trinity tomorrow." He was not completely settled about the call, describing it in the same letter, "The call came two weeks ago, and since then I have been in a wretched state, weighing my desire to stay with the Advent people against my apparent duty to go and work in this larger field . . . serious and prayerful thought . . . has resulted finally in a clear conviction that I ought to go. The Advent people are very much hurt and indignant about it."[13]

As a kind and dutiful priest, he wrote a letter to the Advent Vestry upon his resignation, saying, "never has any rector been privileged to minister to a people more kind and earnest and sympathizing . . . a vestry more united, more cordial, and considerate in every state of intercourse with them. For the Church of the Advent, I feel a love and a care that time can never weaken . . . To the Vestry I render my most hearty thanks . . . but I have been led to see it as my duty to accept a field of labor which has opened, and kept open, before me by the Providence of God."[14]

---

11. Letter from Brooks to William, dated April 9, 1861, Allen, *Life and Letters*, 1:366.

12. Allen, *Life and Letters*, 1:366.

13. Letter from Brooks to his parents, dated November 18, 1861, Allen, *Life and Letters*, 1:374.

14. Letter from Brooks to the Church of the Advent Vestry, November 18, 1861, Allen, *Life and Letters*, 1:375.

Where Faith Holds Wide the Door

MINISTRY AT THE CHURCH OF THE HOLY TRINITY, RITTENHOUSE SQUARE

And so it was that Phillips Brooks, at the age of twenty-six, became the second rector of one of the most prominent churches in Philadelphia—The Church of the Holy Trinity on Rittenhouse Square. His time at Holy Trinity was marked with excitement, growth, engagement, and grief. At Holy Trinity, Brooks grew into a bold, passionate, and powerful preacher, but he also began to develop his own sense of self, justice, and faith as he navigated a country that was divided and then deeply grieving from all the Civil War had taken from them.

His going to Holy Trinity was not without controversy. Advent was angry that he was leaving and felt that he *belonged* to them because they were the first to discover him. The Daily Press hinted at the long-held rumor that Holy Trinity had paid off Advent's loan to compel Brooks to come. In an article dated November 20, 1861, the Daily Press wrote:

> The Philistines have triumphed! Holy Trinity rejoiceth! Advent mourns and refuses to be comforted . . . (Holy Trinity) proposed to relieve Advent of an encumbrance of several thousand dollars, *provided* Books accepted. This we regret to learn that gentleman has done, so that the poor of Advent are left to wander without a shepherd, that the aristocratic attendants of Holy Trinity may be accommodated . . . if he can reconcile the change within his own conscience and God, we have nothing to say. But the finger of suspicion will long point at him as one guided in his holy calling by temporal interests."[15]

Colleagues were jealous, and the parishioners and vestry of Advent were furious with him for leaving. If this bothered Brooks, he never spoke or wrote about it.

In his first year, Brooks remarked on the amount of work required for the position. Though he had prided himself on never re-preaching sermons or preaching extemporaneously (without notes), occasions for both arose. Despite all the work, he loved the church and the people, remarking to William in a letter in January 1862, "I like them more and more the more I see of them. They are kind and cordial and full of will to work."[16] And to

---

15. Article in *The Daily Press*, dated November 20, 1861, Allen, *Life and Letters*, 1:381

16. Letter from Brooks to William, dated January 11, 1862, Allen, *Life and Letters*, 1:390.

his father, he wrote, "I find this new parish all that was promised. There is a great deal of wealth and luxury, but also a large amount of intelligence and refinement as well as earnestness and devotion. The church is all taken, and we are slowly providing for our debt by the sales of the pews."[17]

His father wrote to him warning him against the temptation to fall to pride, "You are in a dangerous situation for a young man." Even though this phenomenal growth would have been the talk of the town and drawn the ire and jealousy of fellow priests in the city, Brooks did not seem to be affected by it. Writing back to his father, he said there was "little chance for a man to get too puffed up . . . I am thankful for all the fruits I see, but they are so out of proportion to the needs and capacities of the field that there is enough to humiliate as well as to elate."[18]

Even though many in the congregation were wealthy, the church also drew people with fewer means. Brooks's heart went out to those in deep need, particularly those experiencing poverty or being marginalized. Writing to his father, "we are doing a large work among the poor, over 200 of them being in our classes and societies. Our meetings are all overcrowded, especially our Wednesday evening lectures."[19] There were rumblings among some of the parishioners as the pews began to fill with different kinds of people, not just the poor, but students and families, and even people of color—all who had not previously attended services at Holy Trinity.

The war was also rumbling around him, but it became personal when his youngest brother, George, decided to enlist as a soldier. In a letter to his mother, George wrote, "I shall try to do all my duty to God and my country. Do not fear for me, but do as you promised you would, and as I hope I have done myself; commit me entirely to God, keeping trust in Him and the blessed Saviour whatever may happen."[20] To the great joy of his mother and with the support of Brooks, George was confirmed just before he left for training. Brooks was both excited and fearful for his brother. Now that the war was in full swing, many of the young men in his congregation had enlisted and left. "Almost all the able-bodied men of my church are off to Harrisburg" he wrote to his mother.[21] There was a part of Brooks that mourned the fact that he could not go and fight for his country. "Very many

---

17. Letter from Brooks to his father, dated March 3, 1862. Allen, *Life and Letters*, 1:390.
18. Letter from Brooks to his father, dated March 12, 1862, Allen, *Life and Letters* 1:395.
19. Allen, *Life and Letters*, 1:395.
20. Letter from George to his mother, Allen, *Life and Letters*, 1:412.
21. Letter from Brooks to his mother, September 15, 1982. Allen, *Life and Letters*, 1:414.

of my congregation have gone, and I suppose I shall have to preach almost entirely to the females..."[22] Then, in late September, Brooks was invited to become a battlefield chaplain at Gettysburg, which he threw himself into. He left services on Sunday evening, traveled to Harrisburg by train, spent three days on the battlefield and in the hospital tents, returned by train for his Wednesday evening lecture (writing it often on the train ride), and back to the battlefield Thursday morning. On Saturday, he returned by train to Philadelphia, writing the remainder of his sermons and Sunday school lessons on the ride. He thrived in the work, knowing he was part of a greater cause and caring for those in need.

THE PHILADELPHIA DIVINITY SCHOOL

During the war, when Virginia Seminary closed, a new divinity school began in Philadelphia, which Brooks helped to establish. In early 1864, the Philadelphia Divinity School invited Brooks to become their Professor of Ecclesiastical History. This call stirred up a long dormant part of Brooks—the dream to work in academia. In *The Life and Letters of Phillips Brooks,* Alexander V. G. Allen talks about this dream. "To be a teacher reappeared before him as the highest, most desirable, the most natural calling of a man in this life."[23] He also tired of the increasing publicity of his life at Holy Trinity. He first mentioned this in a letter to William, dated December 20, 1863: "I have decided . . . to give up my parish, and take the professorship of ecclesiastical history in the Divinity School."[24] In a letter to his father in early January, 1864 he listed several reasons for taking the position, and then ended with "a more personal reason. I need it for myself. In the whirl of this life, I get no time for study. Everything is going out, nothing is coming in . . . I shall do more and get more good in my professor's chair."[25] But he also felt the pull of duty and his love of his parish. "My parish is very dear to me, but this other work is so important . . . I am very much inclined to think it is my duty to accept this call."[26]

---

22. Letter from Brooks to his father, September 19, 1862. Allen, *Life and Letters,* 1:415.

23. Allen, *Life and Letters,* 1:483.

24. Allen, *Life and Letters,* 1:480.

25. Allen, *Life and Letters,* 1:484.

26. Letter from Brooks to William dated January 9, 1962. Allen, *Life and Letters,* 1:485.

Holy Trinity, however, did not share Brooks's enthusiasm for this new call. While Brooks thought it might be easy for them to find another Rector, they could not imagine anyone being able to succeed him as their rector. At the first vestry meeting after he notified them of this call, they passed the following resolution:

> Resolved. That the Vestry of the Church of the Holy Trinity do hereby present their warm, affectionate, and earnest remonstrance to the Rev. Mr. Brooks against any action which would terminate their close and endearing connection with him, and deprive the people of their church and this city of such an element of power as he now possesses; and they add their warm desire that both with reference to his own usefulness and to their spiritual welfare and that of others, the rector will see fit to decline the position which it proposed to offer him.
>
> James Biddle, Secretary of the Vestry.[27]

Other parishioners, former colleagues, and scholars wrote to him with impassioned letters, encouraging him not to take the position. One such letter by his close friend, Rev. CJ Stille, stated, "your withdrawal (is) now a public calamity."[28] Letters from other colleagues alluded to the failures of those who made a similar decision, citing one priest "left one of the most active and influential churches in the city for a professorship ... within two years he told me ... it has been the mistake of his life."[29] These admonitions began to wear on Brooks, who despite his confidence in the pulpit, was also deeply influenced by what others thought of him. If the Divinity School had any opinion, they did not share it, staying silent as the debate continued.

For Holy Trinity, this new development was catastrophic. They were not willing to accept that their beloved and acclaimed rector would leave them. They met as a congregation to discuss the situation and sent a two page letter to Brooks expressing their "painful surprise" and to "take such action ... to avert from the parish so great a calamity as the dissolution of happy relations at present existing between them and their beloved rector."[30] In the letter, they spelled out why he should stay and why, though he could influence students, "the true sphere of usefulness for our pastor is at the

---

27. Vestry Minutes dated January 12, 1864, from The Church of the Holy Trinity archives, Philadelphia. 195–96.

28. Letter from CJ Stille to Brooks, dated January 13, 1864, Allen, *Life and Letters*, 1:488.

29. Allen, *Life and Letters*, 1:489.

30. Allen, *The Life and Letters*, 1:491.

head of this parish . . . It is impossible that we should consent to sever the tie which his ability, devotion, and earnest interest have formed between us, and thereby entail a sorrow which we cannot contemplate without the deepest emotion."[31] They sweetened the deal by offering to give him "certain hours daily, say from 10 am to 3 pm or such hours as he may select, exclusively for his own study."[32] With all this pressure, Brooks acquiesced and declined the professorship, letting go once again of his own desires and leaning in to do what was right. This was a dichotomy within, longing for his own comforts and enjoyment, yet always pulled toward his duty as a priest to the people he served. This was a big loss for Brooks. He grieved it for a time, and then, as he always did, threw himself back into his choice.

SPEAKING OUT AGAINST SLAVERY

Brooks's notoriety as a preacher and orator continued to spread. He was described in the *Philadelphia Press*, "There is something so genuine in Mr. Brook's sermons that we no more feel that we are praising *him* when we are admiring *them* than we do when we admire ripe fruit and pluck it an eat it with relish and feel refreshed by it, that we are praising the soil out of which it grows."[33]

While he grew up in Boston, in a respectable family, where he was taught to take a middle road when it came to the issue of slavery, Brooks found himself drawn to the abolitionists in Philadelphia. His time in Virginia, along with his experiences with the poor and on the battlefields, began to form his own thoughts on slavery, and as the war dragged on, he could not continue holding a neutral position. Despite his father's admonition against him talking publicly on the subject, he began to talk openly about his anti-slavery views.

His first opportunity was in October 1862 at the General Convention of the Episcopal Church in New York. Shocked at the number of clergy who hid behind religion as a reason to not take a stand on the war, he wrote to William, "I agree with you perfectly about the Convention. It's shilly-shallying was disgraceful." But he also encouraged William not to give up on the church. "She's got a thick crust of old-fogyism, but she's alright at the

---

31. Allen, *The Life and Letters*, 1:492.
32. Allen, *The Life and Letters*, 1:492.
33. Allen, *Life and Letters*, 1:513.

core, and I hope will show it yet."[34] Brooks joined the founding of the Union League and whole-heartedly supported Lincoln and the Union troops. He gave speeches and prayers at abolitionist events and worked with Octavius Catto to desegregate the cable cars in Philadelphia. After the Emancipation Proclamation was signed, he called for full citizenship of freed slaves, including the right to vote.

While he had been speaking boldly in the community and in the wider church, he had not yet dared to speak his views from the pulpit. This changed in 1863, following two events that happened back-to-back: President Lincoln signed the Emancipation Proclamation on January 1st, and just a month later, his brother, George, died from typhoid pneumonia at the age of twenty-four in New Bern, North Carolina while serving in the 45th Massachusetts Volunteer Regiment.

As Brooks was celebrating the edict to free all from the tyranny of slavery, word came of his brother George was sick with typhoid pneumonia and then of his death. Brooks returned home to sit in wake and await the return of his father with George's body. In his journal, dated February 16, 1863, Brooks quoted Tennyson:

> Sphere all your lights around, above
> Sleep gentle heavens, before the prow
> Sleep gentle winds, as he sleeps now
> My friend, the brother of my love.[35]

When Brooks returned to Philadelphia, he was still grieving. He wrote to his mother, "I feel like a stranger here among the things that were so familiar only two weeks ago . . . like a strange sort of dream, and it is hard to believe."[36] But the work of a clergyman did not stop for grief, so Brooks carried this grief with him and decided to speak out against the continuation of the war and of the evils of slavery.

The Emancipation Proclamation was the pinnacle of everything Brooks believed was good and true. Ridding the country of the stain of slavery was of the highest spiritual importance to him as well as a moral imperative for the nation. Writing to his brother, William, he said, "If this

---

34. Letter from Brooks to William dated October 24, 1862, Allen, *Life and Letters*, 1:438.

35. Journal entry dated February 16, 1863, quoting Lord Tennyson, *Poem 9 of In Memorium A.H.H.*, London, Edward Moxon, 1850, Allen, *Life and Letters*, 1:438–39.

36. Letter from Brooks to his mother, dated March 3, 1863. Allen, *Life and Letters*, 1:441.

war hadn't done anything else so far, at any rate, it has made us an anti-slavery people, and begin the end of this infernal institution."[37] Following the signing of this proclamation, Brooks preached two significant sermons on slavery. First, delivering a sermon on March 27, 1863, which was designated as *Fast Day*, for all churches. Second, he preached on the occasion of the first national Thanksgiving in November of the same year.

Most churches were bursting with crowds on the day marked *Fast Day*, and Holy Trinity was no different. At this service, Brooks took this opportunity to preach on the evils of slavery, "the greatest sin of all—the blackest stain upon our country and the cause of all the ruin and bloodshed and affliction that have been visited upon our land—the black sin of slavery."[38] While the *Philadelphia Press* praised Brooks for his service, saying, "The congregation listened with the most profound attention and apparently gave a sincere and hearty response to his remarks," there was also friction within his parish about this bold address.[39] Writing to his brother, William, he remarked, "Judge Woods resigned his seat on my vestry and advertised his pew for sale. I'm sorry for he is a pleasant man and has been one of my kindest friends."[40] Brooks, however, would not be swayed. In a reflection by his good friend, The Rev. C.A.L. Richards, described Brooks's reaction. He "quietly disregarded it, went his ways in spite of it . . . his heart never flinched or failed. His light ever shone out clear."[41]

The following November, President Lincoln declared Thanksgiving as a national holiday. A Philadelphia resident and the first woman publisher of a national magazine, Sarah Hale (who also wrote *Mary had a little lamb*), had petitioned three presidents to create this national holiday, but only Lincoln made it so. One of the most widely read and fondly thought of sermons by Brooks during his time in Philadelphia was the sermon he preached on this occasion: "Our Mercies of Reoccupation" based on Jeremiah 16:14–15. In it, Brooks finally decided to speak his mind on the matter.

> You do not expect me, I do not think you want me, to stand here to-day without thanking God that the institution of African

---

37. Letter from Brooks to William, dated October 17, 1863, Allen, *Life and Letters*, 1:462.

38. Sermon for "Fast Day" preached at The Church of the Holy Trinity, Philadelphia on March 27, 1863, Allen, *Life and Letters*, 1:445.

39. Allen, *Life and Letter*, 1:445.

40. Allen, *Life and Letters*, 1:463.

41. Allen, *Life and Letters*, 1:450.

slavery is one big year nearer to its inevitable death . . . To-day, will any man or woman blame us if we stand in the anticipation of certainty, and cry above the opened grave of slavery, that only waits till its corpse be brought to it with the decency its reverend age demands, Thank God! thank God! the hateful thing is dead!

With regard to this whole slavery question . . . I count the possibilities of the question to be sealed up and closed . . . But speaking from the pulpit, putting this question on the highest ground, there is one distinction that belongs to us to draw. We hear so many people, even strong anti-slavery men, talking about the matter—Yes," they say, "Slavery is going fast, and we are glad of it. We shall be better off without it. The country will be richer. The Union will be safer. Our rejoicing is for the white man. It is not for the negro that we care." They make this last proviso in their creed most scrupulously. It seems to me it is a very mean, and low, and selfish one to make. It is for the negro that we care. It is our fault and not his, that he is here. It is our fault, inherited from the fathers, that has kept in most utter bondage, and most cruel bondage too, (I believe nobody doubts that now), generation after generation of men.

We rejoice in emancipation because it is right. We hate slavery because it is wrong. The negro ought to be free. He has a right to be free. God is showing us how to do it, and by His help we are doing it; casting this sin away, and reentering, as He leads us, the high temple of human brotherhood, whence by His grace we will go no more out. That, and that alone, is the true ground to take, the high ground of Duty, which binds the conscience of our people to the cause of freedom.[42]

The reaction of those present, and all those who heard about it (which spread quickly across the city and the national church), was that this was more than just a sermon. His father, who had previously warned against such declarations from the pulpit, asked for "a dozen copies of that sermon," and colleagues from up and down the east coast gave glowing reviews.

LINCOLN'S ASSASSINATION AND THE YEAR ABROAD

As Brooks was preparing his 1865 Easter Sermon, just having completed the Good Friday liturgy in the church, news of President Lincoln's death reached him. Brooks was devastated, having placed all his hope on Lincoln

---

42. Phillips Brooks, *Our Mercies of Reoccupation* sermon preached at The Church of the Holy Trinity, November 26, 1863.

to cure this country's ills and make it the good and equitable place he knew it could be. Whatever Easter sermon Brooks had prepared was promptly laid to the side, and Brooks wrote an eloquent and beautiful eulogy-esque remembrance of Lincoln for all who gathered that day. "My friends," Brooks began, "Easter Day is not what we expected it to be . . . Even when sadness is upon us heavy as it is today; when death in its most terrible personal form has come upon us; when death has dealt to us a most tremendous blow, do we not need Easter Day of all days."[43] He continued, sharing his own feelings about Abraham Lincoln:

> . . . he was the man most distinctly and in the best and truest sense an American . . . His moral character, too, as distinguished above the intellectual. He spoke the words which his nature urged him to speak. Bravely and boldly he told it, no matter how men might differ with him or seek to dissuade him. Where shall we find another that would take his place?[44]

He concluded the sermon, "I believe in my heart that if there be a man who has left on record that he was a Christian man, a servant and follower of Jesus Christ, it is he." Then, he turned to the children in the crowd, "Abraham must be your example and mine, and something of his character must be replicated in us, or we shall be unworthy of our times."[45] The following day, Brooks was asked to open the gathering at the Union League:

> We thank thee that thou didst put into the hearts of this people to choose such a man, so full of goodness and truth and faithfulness, of patience, serenity and composers of such wisdom to perceive the truth and such steadfastness to do it; for the earnestness with which he laid hold upon the great purpose before him and the calm and wise perseverance with which he followed it.[46]

Heading into the busiest time of the year for clergy, Brooks was already tired, and the death of Lincoln only added to his exhaustion. The loss of a personal hero, along with his brother death, and letting go of his dream

---

43. Sermon for Easter Sunday, preached in The Church of the Holy Trinity on April 12, 1865.

44. Sermon for Easter Sunday, preached in The Church of the Holy Trinity on April 12, 1865.

45. Sermon for Easter Sunday, preached in The Church of the Holy Trinity on April 12, 1865.

46. Opening Prayer, The Union League, Philadelphia, Pennsylvania, April 13, 1865, in Allen, *Life and Letters*, 2:13.

of academia, overshadowed any hope he had just a week before. Within Brook's devastating grief, he was languishing. The leadership at Holy Trinity could see all of this, and offered Brooks a year's sabbatical, which he accepted. Without family or obligations and following the tradition of many clergy on sabbaticals at the time, Brooks decided to travel abroad.

His first stop was back in Boston, at Harvard University, for the Commemoration of those lost in the war. He was asked to offer the opening prayer. While there is no written record of the prayer he offered on that day, it profoundly affected those who heard it. "That prayer! O that prayer! It is not too much to say that that prayer was the crowning grace of the Commemoration."[47] An attendee said "that when he saw the name of Mr. Brooks on the programme (sic), he wondered why a young man of whom he'd never heard should be chosen . . . But with the first sentence . . . he found himself listening breathless. He felt he had never heard a living prayer before."[48]

TRAVELS ABROAD

On August 9, 1865, Brooks boarded the steamer *Scotia* of the Cunard Line for England and arrived in the British Isles on August 18th. His year-long journey took him to the places of his roots that he longed to see. He began in England, where his church began, traveled to Germany, where his favorite theologians hailed, then to Constantinople, from where he could witness the whirling dervishes, and finally into the Holy Land, where Paul, John, and Jesus once walked. Writing to his mother, two months into his travels, "They have been the fullest months of my life. Not a day goes by without seeing something I have longed for my whole life to see."[49]

On his thirtieth birthday, December 13, 1865, he camped by the fountain of Nazareth, traveling to the Sea of Galilee the following day. He was inspired in this place where Jesus walked. "The whole country, every hill and valley, seemed marked by his footprints."[50] Just ten days later, on Christmas Eve, Brooks and his companions attend a service in Jerusalem and then rode their horses into Bethlehem. "Before dawn we rode out of the

---

47. Bail, "Harvard's Commemoration Day," 265.
48. Bail, "Harvard's Commemoration Day," 265.
49. Brooks, *Letters of Travel*, 40.
50. Allen, *Life and Letters*, 2:57.

town to the field where they say the shepherds saw the star."[51] They returned and attended service, lasting into the early hours of the morning.

Throughout his life, Brooks had dabbled in writing poems and children's carols, and this experience inspired him to write the text of *O Little Town of Bethlehem*. Three years later, Lewis Redner, his organist, composed *St. Louis* and the carol was completed.[52] Brooks offered the carol to the children as a gift on Christmas Eve 1868 to ease the suffering they had all gone through over the long years of the war. His vision was one of hope that did not shy away from the reality of the world, and a deep appreciation of the light Christ brings in his incarnation to the dark world. Writing to the children he remembered, "when I was standing in the old church at Bethlehem, close to the spot where Jesus was born, when the whole church was ringing hour and hour with the splendid hymns of praise to God, how ... it seemed as if I could hear voices that I knew well, telling each other of the 'wonderful night' of our Saviour's (sic) birth."

BACK IN PHILADELPHIA

He ended his time in Rome and Italy, describing it "so much greater and fuller than I ever dreamed of," and returned to Philadelphia in October, 1866.[53] In his journal, Brooks wrote, "It's rather pleasant to feel myself at ministry again," but he also hinted at being restless and how different the church feels.[54] This was the case for someone who so thoroughly threw himself into everything he did—so deeply immersing himself in the "Old World" that he felt "drearily homesick."[55] Over time, he returned to the busy life and pace of ministering at Holy Trinity.

His first big project was completing the building with the addition of the bell tower. After traveling through Europe and the Holy Land, Brooks had discovered a love of architecture. His ideal church building highlighted the low-church aspects of Protestantism, while also retaining the glory of the early medieval architecture. For Brooks, the tower should be grand, but not pretentious. The Vestry had its own idea of how the bell tower might look, hoping to add a large and impressive spire like neighboring St. Mark's.

---

51. Allen, *Life and Letters*, 2:63.
52. Aspinwall, *A Hundred Years*, 67.
53. Brooks, *Letters of Travel*, 42.
54. Allen, *Life and Letters*, 2:59.
55. Allen, *Life and Letters*, 2:59.

Brooks was adamantly against it. "I have just broken my head against my vestry in an attempt to put a tower harmonious and solid on my church. I have failed."[56] In the end, however, Brooks did not fail, and the tower was built without spire and stands testament today to him, a unique tower among the many spires that dot the skyline in the city.

THE CALL TO TRINITY, BOSTON

While offers from churches throughout the country continued to come in, it was a call from Brooks's hometown of Boston that turned his head. Perhaps the idea of returning to Boston began when he delivered the Commemoration speech at Harvard. Or perhaps it was the invitation to become the head of the Episcopal Divinity School about six months after he returned from his travels, which he turned down. Or perhaps it was his homesickness for his family and familiar things. Whatever the case, when Trinity Boston sent a call to him in April 1868, he took his time before turning them down.

Holy Trinity breathed a sigh of relief, but Trinity, Boston, was devastated. In a letter to Brooks, the senior warden wrote, "You're putting an end to all our hopes came duly to hand . . . what shall we do I have not the least idea."[57] In the end, Trinity, Boston decided to wait a year and try to call Brooks again. This was a significant sacrifice for them, as it was not easy or cost effective to leave a church open without a rector for such a long time, but they knew who they wanted.

In this year, Brooks found himself petitioned by college friends, colleagues from Boston, and most intensely from his parents and brothers. All this pressure made him finally give in. On July 29, 1869, Brooks wrote his resignation to his dear friend, Lemuel Coffin, whose house he spent nearly every Saturday evening for dinner. "At last, with great sorrow, I send you my resignation . . . You don't agree with me, but I beg you to believe me honest and sincere in my desire to do what is right. I have given it thought, carefulness, and prayer, and have tried to decide it in God's fear."[58]

After so many attempts from so many places to call Brooks away from Holy Trinity, the church would not fight this call. On July 31, the vestry met to accept his resignation. He was never expected to stay as long as he

---

56. Letter to C.A.L. Richards in Letter from Brooks to C.A.L. Richards. Allen, *Life and Letters*, 2:63.

57. Allen, *Life and Letters*, 2:81.

58. Allen, *Life and Letters*, 2:104.

did or even end up in Philadelphia, but Philadelphia was the fertile ground for so many of Brooks's accomplishments and renown. Almost ten years exactly after first arriving, The Rev. Phillips Brooks ended his chapter in Philadelphia, leaving a lasting legacy.

BIBLIOGRAPHY

Allen, Alexander V. G. *The Life and Letters of Phillips Brooks*. Vol. 1. New York: Dutton, 1900.
———. *The Life and Letters of Phillips Brooks*. Vol. 2. New York: Dutton, 1900.
Aspinwall, Marguerite. *A Hundred Years in this House*. Philadelphia: The Rectors, Churchwardens and Vestrymen of The Church of the Holy Trinity, 1956.
Bail, Hamilton Vaughan. "Harvard's Commemoration Day July 21, 1865." *The New England Quarterly* 15.2 (June 1942) 256–79.
Brooks, Phillips. *Letters of Travel*. Vol. 2. New York: Dutton, 1920.
———. *Our Mercies of Reoccupation*. Sermon Preached at The Church of the Holy Trinity, November 26, 1863.
———. Sermon preached Easter Day, April 12, 1865, The Church of the Holy Trinity, Philadelphia.
Vestry Minutes from the Archives of The Church of the Holy Trinity, vol. 1. Philadelphia: The Church of the Holy Trinity. 1857–present.

4

How Still

The Participatory Poetry and Theology of "O Little Town of Bethlehem"

Karen Swallow Prior

THE STORY BEHIND "O Little Town of Bethlehem" is well-known to anyone familiar with Phillips Brooks. During his tenure as rector of the Church of the Holy Trinity in Philadelphia (1862–69), Brooks spent a year traveling abroad (1865–66). This was the year after the end of the Civil War, and Brooks had stood on the side of abolition, delivering sermons commemorating the life and death of Abraham Lincoln and the lives lost in the war. In the aftermath of loss and weariness, Brooks needed time away. During his trip, Brooks visited the Holy Land. While in Jerusalem on Christmas Eve of 1865, Brooks journeyed two hours on horseback to Bethlehem, passing on his way the field where the shepherds are said to have heard the message of the angels.[1]

Three Christmases later, back home in his home church in Philadelphia, Brooks drew on this experience to write the poem that would become the hymn that the world would come to know and love. He composed the verses for the Sunday School children of the Church of the Holy Trinity. The congregation's organist, Lewis Henry Redner, put the words to

---

1. Leland Ryken, *Journey to Bethlehem*, 29.

music, and the carol was first performed at the church's Sunday service on December 27, 1868.[2]

The publication history of the hymn is complicated. The text of the song (with its original five stanzas) was first published in 1870 and then appeared with its musical arrangement in 1874.[3] The original text of the poem had five stanzas, including one Brooks omitted nearly immediately after performing it; this four-stanza version is the one most often published and performed today.[4] Some hymnals include an additional stanza not written by Brooks. Additionally, the song has been set to different musical scores, offering even more variations. (More on the original music is below.) Today, "O Little Town of Bethlehem" is one of the most popular Christmas carols. By Hymnary.org's count, it consistently appears in around 50 percent of church hymnals (peaking in 1996 at 63 percent).[5] In 2022, it ranked at number nine out of thirty in *Classic FM*'s list of top Christmas carols,[6] and was number seven the previous year in a list compiled by Lifeway, the retail arm of the Southern Baptist Convention.[7]

The text under discussion in this essay is Brooks's final four-stanza version.

> 1. O little town of Bethlehem,   1
>   How still we see thee lie;
> Above thy deep and dreamless sleep
>   The silent stars go by:
> Yet in thy dark streets shineth   5
>   The everlasting Light;
> The hopes and fears of all the years
>   Are met in thee to-night.

---

2. "O Little Town of Bethlehem." n.d. Hymnology Archive. https://www.hymnologyarchive.com/o-little-town-of-bethlehem.

3. "O Little Town of Bethlehem."

4. "O Little Town of Bethlehem."

5. "O Little Town of Bethlehem."

6. "The 30 Greatest Christmas Carols of All Time." n.d. Classic FM. https://www.classicfm.com/discover-music/occasions/christmas/nations-top-30-christmas-carols/.

7. "Top 15 Christmas Songs for Churches | Lifeway." n.d. www.lifeway.com. https://www.lifeway.com/en/articles/research-top-15-christmas-songs-for-churches.

2. For Christ is born of Mary;
   And gathered all above,					10
While mortals sleep, the angels keep
   Their watch of wondering love.
O morning stars, together
   Proclaim the holy birth;
And praises sing to God the King,				15
   And peace to men on earth.

3. How silently, how silently,
   The wondrous gift is given!
So God imparts to human hearts
   The blessings of His heaven.				20
No ear may hear His coming,
   But in this world of sin,
Where meek souls will receive Him still,
   The dear Christ enters in.

4. O holy Child of Bethlehem,					25
   Descend to us, we pray;
Cast out our sin, and enter in,
   Be born in us to-day.
We hear the Christmas angels
   The great glad tidings tell;					30
O come to us, abide with us,
   Our Lord Emmanuel.

Written, as already noted, for the children of the church, "O Little Town of Bethlehem" employs (with some variation) the common meter, more specifically, the ballad measure, which is used in many popular English songs. This meter consists of four lines that alternate between iambic tetrameter (four metrical feet per line) and iambic trimeter (three metrical feet per line). More specifically, the carol features the ballad quatrain, each stanza consisting of two quatrains that follow the rhyme scheme ABCB. Such an interlocking rhyme scheme invites more sustained attention to the narrative flow than the rhyming couplets found in other popular hymns and carols such as "Hark, The Herald Angels Sing" (1739) and "We Three Kings" (1857), for example. The rhyme scheme and other sound devices that will be detailed below serve to make the poem easier to learn and memorize, particularly for children, Brooks's original primary audience.

The long tradition of the ballad carries with it echoes of Anglo-Saxon alliteration and stress-based verse (which would later be replaced by syllable-based measures).⁸ In addition to the meter that flows with ease, most of the words in the lyrics are short, simple, and familiar. Few words in the song have more than two syllables. The only two words that have four syllables—everlasting and Emmanuel—are sweetly melodious, and yet they carry significant theological import. As an early publisher of Brooks's papers said of the hymn, "It is an exquisitely simple thing, and yet one feels behind the words the existence of a great soul, meditating on the mystery of the divine revelation."⁹

The ballad form—generally defined as a narrative song or poem that consists of short stanza—has a long history in the English folk tradition. Whether or not ballads ought to be considered first as texts or songs is a matter of debate among scholars across disciplines.¹⁰ This debate evidences, as one scholar observes,

> . . . how the English popular ballad, dating from the fourteenth century or earlier, preserves traces of archaic forms now obscure. One thing that is clear is that its measure, rhythm, and general pattern are simple and repetitive, suggestive of its ancient origins from a largely illiterate society wherein songs and other mnemonic devices allowed for easy memorization of important events, histories, and legends.¹¹

It is not the purpose of this paper to discuss the musical arrangements of the carol, but rather to examine "O Little Town of Bethlehem" as a work of poetry. Even intended originally as a mere song for Sunday School children meant to be performed in a local church's worship service, "O Little Town of Bethlehem" possesses poetic brilliance so immense, it could not be confined to that humble beginning.

Modern ears tend to be most highly attuned to meter and rhyme, and as already noted, "O Little Town of Bethlehem," as a traditional ballad, employs these literary devices expertly. But several other poetic devices contribute to the literary art of the text.

---

8. "Ballad Measure in Print—UCSB English Broadside Ballad Archive." n.d. Ebba. english.ucsb.edu. https://ebba.english.ucsb.edu/page/ballad-measure-in-print#.

9. "O Little Town of Bethlehem." n.d. Encyclopedia of Greater Philadelphia. https://philadelphiaencyclopedia.org/essays/o-little-town-of-bethlehem/.

10. "Ballad Measure in Print—UCSB English Broadside Ballad Archive." n.d. Ebba. english.ucsb.edu. https://ebba.english.ucsb.edu/page/ballad-measure-in-print#.

11. "Ballad Measure in Print—UCSB English Broadside Ballad Archive." n.d. Ebba. english.ucsb.edu. https://ebba.english.ucsb.edu/page/ballad-measure-in-print#.

One of these devices is internal rhyme, which occurs frequently in the poem. In addition to adding to the musicality of the poem, internal rhymes (rhymes which occur within the same line), like all repeated sounds, help make the poem easier to remember. Internal rhymes are found frequently within the poem:

Line 2: *we see thee*

Line 3: *deep, sleep*

Line 7: *hears, years*

Line 11: *sleep, keep*

Line 12: *of, love*

Line 15: *sing, King*

Line 17: *how silently, silently*

Line 19: *imparts, hearts*

Line 21: *ear, hear*

Line 23: *will, still*

Line 27: *sin, in*

Line 31: *us, us*

The internal rhymes of lines seventeen and thirty-one are also identical rhymes; line seventeen (*how silently, how silently*) also employs anaphora (successive repetition). Line thirty-one uses epistrophe, the successive repetition of a word or phrase at the end of a grammatical unit. Repetitions of words and phrases like these achieve a litany-like effect which is exceedingly suitable for a song of worship.

When internal rhyme occurs within, or especially at the end of, each of two halves of a line (as occurs particularly clearly in lines nineteen, twenty-seven, and thirty-one), the form echoes the half-line that characterizes Anglo-Saxon or Old English poetry. Poetry of the Anglo-Saxon period (450–1066) relies not on rhyme but on alliteration. Anglo-Saxon poetry is also characterized by units called half-lines, each of which are connected by alliteration of key words. Alliteration occurs when the initial consonant sounds are repeated near one another, particularly, but not necessarily, in the same line. Middle and Modern English came to favor rhyme over alliteration—representing, essentially, a shift from repetition of the beginning sound of two words to repetition of the end sound. Nevertheless, alliteration remains common in modern poetry (as well as in branding products), and examples of its effective use abound in "O Little Town of Bethlehem":

Line 2: *still, see*

Line 3: *deep, dreamless*

Lines 2–8: *thee, thy, the, thy, the, the, the, thee*

Line 4: *silent, stars*

Line 12: *watch, wondering*

Line 18: *gift, given*

Line 21: *hear, his*

Line 23: *souls, still*

Line 28: *be, born*

Line 30: *great, glad*

Line 30: *tidings tell*

As already mentioned, alliteration is most obvious when the repeating sounds are in the same line. Yet, the ear hears such repetition wherever it occurs closely, even if in a subsequent line, such as in these lines from the song:

Lines 14–16: *proclaim, praises, peace*

Lines 19–20: *human, hearts, his, heaven*

Rhyme and alliteration are the most easily recognized sound repetition in a poem. However, other more subtle forms of repetition contribute just as much to the effect of the poem in ways that can easily go unnoticed. Consonance, like alliteration, repeats a consonant sound in nearby words, but in this case not only in the beginning of the words. Consonance (excluding the exact rhymes) can be heard in:

Lines 1–2: li*ttl*e, s*t*ill

Line 5: ye*t*, s*t*ree*t*s

Line 6: ever*l*asting, *l*ight

Line 8: me*t*, *t*onigh*t*

Line 11: whi*l*e, morta*l*s, s*l*eep, ange*l*s

Line 30: *g*reat, *g*lad, tidings

Line 32: *L*ord, Emmanu*e*l

An even softer, more subtle poetic sense is achieved through assonance, the repetition of vowel sounds in non-rhyming words.

> Line 4: s*i*lent, b*y*
>
> Lines 5–6: y*e*t, shin*e*th, *e*verlasting
>
> Line 10: *a*nd, g*a*thered, *a*ll, *a*bove
>
> Lines 13–14: *O*, pr*o*claim, h*o*ly
>
> Line 19: g*i*ft, *i*s, g*i*ven
>
> Line 20: bl*e*ssings, h*e*aven
>
> Line 22: *i*n, th*i*s, s*i*n
>
> Line 25: *O*, h*o*ly
>
> Line 26: d*e*scend, w*e*

Assonance and consonance—wonderfully described as "fragments of melodious or euphonious phrases"—contribute to the overall effect of the poem by creating "temporary, ephemeral patterns in a given line or phrase that dissipate as quickly as they emerge."[12] Such sounds are always beautiful, but their beauty here is not mere aestheticism, but rather serves to reflect the hymn's truth and goodness as part of an integrated whole.

The cumulative effect of all of these sound devices—meter, rhyme, alliteration assonance, and consonance—helps to explain the inherent musicality of Brooks's poem—even before it was set to music by Redner. Redner's account of this part of the carol's story adds to the mystery of the poem's mesmerizing power:

> As Christmas of 1868 approached, Mr. Brooks told me that he had written a simple little carol for the Christmas Sunday-school service, and he asked me to write the tune to it. The simple music was written in great haste and under great pressure. We were to practice it on the following Sunday. Mr. Brooks came to me on Friday, and said, 'Redner, have you ground out that music yet to "O Little Town of Bethlehem"?' I replied, 'No,' but that he should have it by Sunday. On the Saturday night previous my brain was all confused about the tune. I thought more about my Sunday-school

---

12. "What Are Assonance and Consonance? | Definition & Examples." 2020. College of Liberal Arts. December 3, 2020. https://liberalarts.oregonstate.edu/wlf/what-are-assonance-and-consonance#.

lesson than I did about the music. But I was roused from sleep late in the night hearing an angel-strain whispering in my ear, and seizing a piece of music paper I jotted down the treble of the tune as we now have it, and on Sunday morning before going to church I filled in the harmony. Neither Mr. Brooks nor I ever thought the carol or the music to it would live beyond that Christmas of 1868.

Redner's arrangement remains the tune most frequently sung, particularly in America. However, Ralph Vaugh Williams later set "O Little Town of Bethlehem" to his adaptation of the traditional folk tune "Forest Green" and published this arrangement in a hymnal in 1906.[13] This the arrangement usually used in England and other countries. Other versions have also been published and performed for more than one hundred years.

A poem does not consist solely, of course, of its sound (Lewis Carroll's "Jabberwocky" notwithstanding). A well-crafted poem joins sound and sense effectively, and the art of Brooks's hymn is in doing exactly this. The sounds support the images and ideas of the poem, from its mood to its theological content.

Much of the mood of the poem is carried by the sounds of the words, as discussed above (and later, of course, the music). But words like *still* (which will be discussed more below), *dreamless, sleep, silent,* and *dark* immediately evoke a quiet, reverent tone that only builds throughout the poem.

Mood is created not only by sound but by imagery as well. Recurring images of light and darkness permeate the poem, from the dark streets shining (line 5) to the *Everlasting Light* (line 6), to the light evoked by the *morning stars* (lines 4 and 13). Further imagery is found in the alternating sense of up and down, descent and ascent, movement suggested by the mention in various lines of the stars, angels, and heaven above, to the streets and earth below to which Christ descends.

But the most dominant form of imagery in the poem centers on sound and silence. A form of the word *silent* occurs three times, along with words that connote the same idea, such as *still* and *sleep*. The sense of silence that so strongly characterizes the hymn suggests a paradox with the primacy within Chrisitan theology of the Word of God being spoken and heard. In Genesis, God speaks creation into existence. He speaks to Adam and Eve in the Garden of Eden. In Exodus, God speaks to Moses. He whispers to Elijah in 1 Kings. In the books of Joel and Amos, God utters and roars. Acts

---

13. "O Little Town of Bethlehem."

3:21 says that God spoke through the mouths of his prophets. The Word Incarnate comes quietly, a paradox found in both the biblical narrative and conveyed in this song. "O Little Town of Bethlehem" begins with images of stillness and silence, imagery reinforced by the tune to which it is sung. "No ear may hear His coming" (line 21), yet the stars proclaim his birth and sing praises without words (lines 14–15). Finally, in the last stanza, "We hear the Christmas angels / The great glad tidings tell" (lines 29–30).

Altogether, the recurring images in the poem offer a series of paradoxes: the paradox of light coming through darkness, of a transcendent God becoming immanent, of hearing the presence of the Lord amid silence. These paradoxes reflect the ultimate paradox of the Incarnation, of God becoming human, and of the very meaning of the last word in the poem, *Emmanuel—God with us*.

The imagery helps to carry the theological substance of the poem. "O Little Town of Bethlehem" is a Christmas carol, thus, naturally, its theme centers on the nativity and the incarnation, events central to both the Christian faith and the liturgical calendar of the church as all Christmas hymns do. Yet, the imagery that is absent from the song also gives its theological content greater weight. This poem has no shepherds, no wise men, no manger or inn, and not even Joseph. The lines offer us only Christ, Mary, stars, and angels—of course, Bethlehem.

Not by Brooks's choice, of course, but even the single word, "Bethlehem," is remarkable for both its musicality and its meaning. For the Christian, the connotations carried by this geographical place are immediate: it is the birth of the Messiah, prophesied in the Old Testament (Micah 5:2), but first mentioned in Genesis 35:16–19 as Rachel died outside the village as she and her family were journeying there. Numerous mentions of Bethlehem are woven throughout the Old Testament, culminating in the narrative of Christ's birth as described in Matthew, Luke, and John.

Ironically, the fact that the hymn is an address to Bethlehem—a literary device called apostrophe, an address to an absent person or inanimate object—made the song questionable at first in terms of its appropriateness for inclusion in a worship hymnal. However, if we understand apostrophe to be a figure of speech, not a literalism, one recognizes how Bethlehem functions in the song, even before the shift in the final stanza to address the Child of Bethlehem. Moreover, if we consider Bethlehem to be a form of metonymy, then the song can be considered an address to God.

Metonymy is a figure of speech in which an adjunct stands for the whole. Here, Bethlehem is clearly associated with the birth of Christ and, therefore, Christ. Metonymy is a figure of speech which, Janet Martin Soskice explains, "points[s] directly to the absent term." Unlike metaphor, which suggests, casts new visions and associations, metonymy and its close cousin synecdoche "function as oblique reference," and are "primarily ornamental ways of naming."[14] Understood as a trope that works in this particular way, one can recognize the apostrophe to Bethlehem as a figurative way to worship God.

Even so, Bethlehem does refer to and function as a literal place within the song, a very particular place that Brooks went to at a very particular time in his life and in history. As Brooks's correspondence shows, being in Bethlehem was a deeply moving spiritual experience, one that connected him not only to that place but to his church back home.

> I remember especially on Christmas Eve, when I was standing in the old church at Bethlehem, close to the spot where Jesus was born, when the whole church was ringing hour after hour with the splendid hymns of praise to God, how again and again it seemed as if I could hear voices that I knew well, telling each other of the "Wonderful Night" of the Saviour's birth, as I heard them a year before; and I assure you I was glad to shut my ears for a while and listen to the more familiar strains that came wandering to me halfway round the world."[15]

At the time of Brooks's visit, Bethlehem was near the end of its Ottoman era, a period of about four hundred years, during most of which the village was ruled by the Ottoman Empire. The first half of the nineteenth century had been marked by outbreak of disease, along with revolts and rebellions, largely over taxes, unemployment and compulsory military service. The second half of the century, however, saw a number of efforts at reform by the Ottoman government, which resulted in building and growth throughout Palestine, including the founding of new churches in Bethlehem. Brooks's visit took place in the middle of the years during which numerous new Christian churches, schools, and ministries were being built, and the vast majority of the population was Christian. The various

---

14. Janet Martin Soskice, *Metaphor and Religious Language*, 57.

15. "O Little Town of Bethlehem—Notes on the Carol." n.d. www.hymnsandcarolsofchristmas.com.

factions and denominations of Christians engaged in continual disputes, however, over ownership and care of various holy sites.[16]

Yet, all this tumult, too, seemed stilled during Brooks's Christmas visit to Bethlehem. He had left on this journey following the death of the American leader in whom hope for the nation's peace had been placed. He found in Bethlehem the birthplace of the one in whom our only true hope—not only for nations but for all of humanity—is found. For, as John Inge argues in *A Christian Theology of Place*, "once divine disclosure has happened in a particular location, it remains associated with that place."[17]

After returning to his war-ravaged homeland, Brooks still carried the experience of his time in Bethlehem so intensely that he was inspired to express his experience there in a poem. He carried the place with him, it carried him, and, in return, he wanted to bring that place back to the community in his home church.

The concept of place is crucial throughout the Bible, but recent years have brought renewed attention to the importance of place in modern theological understanding. The theology of place is particularly compelling in these current days because globalization, migration, and dispersion have fostered rootlessness, particularly in industrialized societies. Moreover, the disenchantment of the "secular age" diagnosed by Charles Taylor has flattened our understanding of the holy and the sacred, including physical and geographical places. As Inge states, the incarnation itself "affirms the importance of the particular, and therefore of place, in God's dealings with humanity." Inge explains that throughout the Bible, particularly in the Old Testament, "the narrative supports a three-way relationship between God, people and place in which all three are essential."[18] Indeed, "places are the seat of relations and of meeting and activity between God and the world."[19]

In centering on Bethlehem, Brooks's poem gestures toward a theology of place. The place of Bethlehem, as described in Brooks's correspondence and in the text of the poem, is a particular geographical spot, one rooted in human history and time. The Bethlehem that Brooks experienced is "little" and had "dark streets" upon which "silent stars" shined. As already mentioned, Brooks also relayed home that he visited the field outside Bethlehem where the shepherds are said to have encountered the angels announcing

---

16. https://thisweekinpalestine.com/bethlehem-in-the-last-century-of-ottoman-rule.
17. Inge, *Theology of Place*, 82.
18. Inge, *Theology of Place*, x.
19. Inge, *Theology of Place*, 68.

Christ's birth. This, too, is an event that happened in a particular place and time. But it is not limited only to that particular place and time, for the poem says, using the present tense and the first person, "We hear the Christmas angels / The great glad tidings tell" (lines 30–31), too. Brooks's presence at the birthplace of Jesus during Christmas, in the immediate aftermath of the long years of violence, hatred, and mass killing that had taken place back home makes the peace, stillness, and joy he experienced in Bethlehem stand out in even sharper relief. Such encounters, Inge observes, become "built into the story of the place for the Christian community as well as the individual, and this is how places become designated as holy."[20] It is not only how they are designated as holy, but also how that designation is remembered and preserved, as Brooks's hymn does.

This background to the hymn is part, not only of its origin story, but also its mythology and its place in America's religious and cultural history. In a 1999 article in *The Atlantic* on poetry and memory, particularly the role memory has played in forging America's identity as a people, poet Robert Pinsky discusses this aspect of the song, writing,

> What gives these lines their mysterious charge is buried memory; Brooks, best known for his famous sermon on the Civil War dead, wrote his Christmas carol when, after the war, many little towns of the North and the South were unnaturally silent, because so many of the young men were gone. 'The hopes and fears of all the years' involve the Republic itself, and in that context the town's 'deep and dreamless sleep,' beneath the silent stars, is the more unsettling precisely because it is dreamless, and therefore deathlike.[21]

The poem shifts in the second half, Leland Ryken points out, and "leaves behind the literal Bethlehem to a spiritual place of becoming."[22] By the final stanza, the poem becomes a prayer comprised of "six petitions," Ryken observes[23]—*descend, cast out, enter in, be born, come, abide*—concluding with the name of the Lord that evokes His place: *with us*.

The literal and metaphorical connection between Bethlehem and the Child of Bethlehem is suggested early in the poem with the word *still* of line 2. *Still* is an example of zeugma, a figure of speech in which a word applies to two other words in different senses. On the surface, it is, of course, the

---

20. Inge, *Theology of Place*, 90.
21. Pinsky, "Poetry and American Memory."
22. Ryken, *Journey to Bethlehem*, 30.
23. Ryken, *Journey to Bethlehem* 30.

town that lies still. Yet, the image also suggests the stillness of the sleeping Christ child. (Interestingly, this is a description previously popularized by another Christmas carol, "Silent Night, Holy Night," written in 1818 and translated into English in 1859 by another Episcopal priest, John Freeman Young, just a few years before Brooks wrote his hymn.) The personification of Bethlehem certainly invites the song's description of its "deep and dreamless sleep," words which, again as aptly apply, implicitly, to the Christ child. *Still* most obviously describes the quietness of the town (or the child), but, again, functioning as zeugma, it also carries the meaning of *now*. The meaning of Bethlehem and the incarnation of Christ are ever present, an actual historical event of two thousand years ago, but not merely that. The meaning of Bethlehem then is present now, *still*.

This zeugma, as indeed the entire hymn, points to the way in which Bethlehem participates in God by reflecting his eternal presence, his peace, and his "everlasting Light." Indeed, the final two lines of the first stanza point more explicitly to the doctrine of participation.

Participation, according to Andrew Davison "rests in perceiving all things in relation to God, not only as their source but also as their goal, and as the origin of all form and character."[24] Pinsky's insight that "the hopes and fears of all the years" which are met in Bethlehem—in the place the Word became flesh, where God is with us—were most immediately those hopes and fears caused by the ravages of the Civil War and the hopes of the dream of America that preceded and followed that war is important. And yet, as a minister of the gospel of Christ, Brooks knew that the hopes and fears of all humanity in *all* our years represent much more than the particular moment in history that marked his own life and country, albeit so traumatically and seemingly irreparably. It is, ultimately, all of humanity's nature as both fallen and reflective of the divine image that is "met" in the coming of Christ in Bethlehem.

"The hopes and fears of all the years" serve as metonymy for all of human experience and history being "met in thee," a participation of humankind in Christ. Such participation is a significant theological point later for the apostle Paul who, Michael Gorman shows, expresses a participatory understanding when he writes of "being in" or "being with" Christ.[25] *In*, in particular is key to participation, according to Gorman: "'In' language is a spatial idiom that signifies a relational reality that is both personal and

---

24. Davison, *Participation in God*, 1.
25. Gorman, *Participating in Christ*, 3.

corporate, both 'vertical' and 'horizontal', both local and universal."[26] Brooks conveys this theological insight marvelously and simply in the hymn with the plea addressed to Christ to "enter in" and "be born in us" (lines 27–28).

Participatory theology distinguishes between God and creation, as Davison explains: "God is not one more being among beings."[27] Understanding Bethlehem as a created thing in and of itself and as something that participates in Christ as the hymn depicts suggests the way in which *we* might participate in him, too. The stillness of Bethlehem sung of in the second line is echoed, fulfilled—and met—by the declaration in line 25 that meek souls receive the child of Bethlehem *still*.

Poetry, too, is a participatory form. Its art relies on the participation of ear and eye, sound and image, all reflections in our human nature of our likeness to our Creator. Our bodies are the *place* wherein Christ meets us, and is born in us, so that we may participate in him.

BIBLIOGRAPHY

Davison, Andrew. *Participation in God: A Study in Christian Doctrine and Metaphysics*. Cambridge: Cambridge University Press, 2020.
Gorman, Michael, J. *Participating in Christ: Explorations in Paul's Theology and Spirituality*. Grand Rapids: Baker Academic, 2019.
Inge, John. *A Christian Theology of Place*. Explorations in Practical, Pastoral, and Empirical Theology. Oxfordshire, UK: Routledge, 2003.
Pinsky, Robert. "Poetry and American Memory." *The Atlantic* (October 1, 1999). https://www.theatlantic.com/magazine/archive/1999/10/poetry-and-american-memory/377805/.
Ryken, Leland. *Journey to Bethlehem: A Treasury of Classic Christmas Devotionals*. Wheaton, IL: Crossway, 2023.
Soskice, Janet Martin. *Metaphor and Religious Language*. Oxford: Clarendon, 1985.

---

26. Gorman, *Participating in Christ*, 5.
27. Davison, *Participation in God*, 2.

Phillips Brooks as a baby with his mother, Mary Ann Phillips Brooks: *carte-de-visite* (card photograph), undated. Phillips Brooks and Brooks family papers, MS Am 2022 (Box 10: 202g). Houghton Library, Harvard University. Photo in the public domain.

Phillips Brooks and family: photograph, 1860. Phillips Brooks and Brooks family papers, MS Am 2022 (Box 9: 2020). Houghton Library, Harvard University. Photo in the public domain.

Phillips Brooks with brothers: *carte-de-visite* (card photograph), tintype, undated. Phillips Brooks and Brooks family papers, MS Am 2022 (Box 10: 202h). Houghton Library, Harvard University. Photo in the public domain.

Phillips Brooks: cabinet photographs, undated. Phillips Brooks and Brooks family papers, MS Am 2022 (Box 10: 202c). Houghton Library, Harvard University. Photo in the public domain.

5

Glory Breaks

Brooks's Influence on Trinity Church in the City of Boston

Cynthia E. Staples and Morgan S. Allen

THE MAIN, WEST DOORS of Church of the Holy Trinity, Rittenhouse Square (Holy Trinity), open to the park space where Philadelphia businesspeople meet colleagues and take their lunch; where neighbors walk strollers and carry grocery bags; where the impoverished find shade and rest; and where tourists make their way from a nearby hotel to City Hall and the historic sites further east. Its architecture prefers neo-Romanesque sturdiness to neo-Gothic spires, a purposeful step away from high church Anglicanism toward what the twenty-first century might identify as a *seeker-friendly* design. Following suit, Holy Trinity's nave-long side galleries and its absence of deep transepts present an interior nearly as much auditorium as church; its apse, with precious little room for an altar, prioritizes oratorical delivery over sacramental celebration.

Phillips Brooks began ministry as Holy Trinity's Rector in 1862, in that building scarcely three years. Seven years later, Brooks accepted the call to serve as Rector of Trinity Church in the City of Boston (Trinity), and his Philadelphia experience surely shaped his vision for what would become Trinity's third home. Rather than inheriting a location and a space, in Boston Brooks could steer decisions about where the congregation should convene, about what styles should shape its sanctuary, and about what its artistry should speak. The achievement he led would launch the Richardsonian-Romanesque architectural epoch, advance the American Art-and-Crafts movement, and inspire a large and vital congregation.

Architect H.H. Richardson, artist John La Farge, the parish's benefactors, and Brooks thoughtfully chose Trinity's details. Their enduring accomplishment expresses both their ideals and ambition, as well as the limits of their season's social, political, and cultural progressivism. Through sermons, letters, and congregational records, this short paper explores the history of Trinity's parish and its current building, plumbs its creators' biographies for hints of their intentions, and reflects on the building's ongoing witness and its congregation's constantly renewing vocation.

MOVING TO COPLEY SQUARE

During the February 9, 1877, ceremonies opening Trinity Church's new home in the City of Boston, Phillips Brooks's Philadelphia predecessor, the Reverend A.H. Vinton, preached the building's consecration, and the project's chief architect, H. H. Richardson, lectured on *the edifice*. In a small volume published to commemorate the occasion, Trinity's vestry also included the *Historical Sermon* Brooks preached the following Sunday. In that February 11 address, Brooks cast his vision for the building just completed:

> [This] noble structure shall speak the genius of the architect. Its glowing walls declare the artist's inspiration. Its unshaken solidity proclaim the builder's skill and care, but only the gratitude of the people's hearts and the good work that shall be done here, can rightly honor the devotion of those who so long have been the wise and willing servants of the parish.[1]

Founded in 1733, Trinity was Boston's third Anglican congregation, following King's Chapel (1686) and Christ Church (1723), which would later become Old North Church. Trinity's congregation first met in two different buildings, built successively on the same Summer Street site in the area now known as Downtown Crossing. Brooks's *Historical Sermon* recalls the first building, consecrated April 15, 1734, as made "of wood, ninety feet long and sixty broad, [the] old pictures of it [showing] us an exterior of such exemplary plainness, as would delight the souls of those who grudge

---

1. Trinity Church, Boston, *Consecration Services*, 47.

the House of God the touch of beauty."[2] Vinton's sermon describes the second building, consecrated on November 11, 1829, as "the massive granite pile we all remember. Although [that Gothic-styled church] was not old, [it] never could have seemed new."[3]

In 1869, at thirty-four years old, Brooks accepted the call to serve as Trinity's Rector. While, earlier in his life, he—by his own accounting—had failed miserably as a teacher at the Boston Latin School (his alma mater),[4] Brooks returned to his hometown as a renowned lecturer and preacher, his sermon eulogizing Abraham Lincoln having stirred international attention. Brooks's arrival at Trinity confirmed his popularity, and he promptly renewed the congregation's Christian education, grew its worship services, and increased its mission work in the city.[5]

As the congregation's life inside the Summer Street church teemed, the surrounding neighborhood commercialized. Brooks recognized that Trinity's parishioners, including foundational families essential to the congregation's social and financial capital, were moving away to more exclusively (and exclusive) residential areas. In response, Brooks convinced the vestry to purchase land in a new location: the Back Bay, a pre-planned neighborhood founded upon a backfilled section of the Charles River basin. After charting this course and securing the new property, The Great Fire of 1872 destroyed Trinity's extant campus, consuming the congregation's timber, stone, and any remaining dissent about the move.[6] The site selected for the next Trinity would set the church on Copley Square. One year before Trinity's consecration, the original Museum of Fine Arts, Boston, opened its grand doors on the site now home to the Fairmont Copley Plaza Hotel. In the decade following, Trustees of the Boston Public Library located the library's enduring home across the Square, completing this assembly of letters, art, and faith.[7] In an arrangement with echoes of Holy Trinity's setting on Rittenhouse Square, this new park space[8] and its surrounding communities brought a broad collection of neighbors and tourists, those busy with

2. Trinity Church, Boston. *Consecration Services*, 28.
3. Trinity Church, Boston. *Consecration Services*, 18.
4. Allen, *Life and Letters of Phillips Brooks*, 1:115–17.
5. Trinity Church, Boston. *Guidebook*, 7.
6. Allen, *Life and Letters*, 2:132–34.
7. Paine, "Chairman of the Building Committee," 44.
8. Copley Square—at the time of this writing, under construction for a significant redevelopment—has taken many forms and served many different purposes.

professions and those suffering from poverty, to Trinity's doorstep. Brooks aspired a building where he could preach to the welcome of them all.

SHAPING SACRED SPACE

In the *Historical Sermon*, Brooks continues:

> We are a parish. We will not degenerate and dissipate into an audience. Very sacred is our relation to each other. But I know that you will more than accept under the great, glowing, all-embracing hospitality of this bounteous roof, you will enthusiastically assert, that such a Church as this, has no right to exist, or to think that it exists, for any limited company who owns its pews. It would not be a Christian parish if it harbored such a thought. No, let the world come in. Let all men hear, if they will, the truths we love.[9]

Architect Henry Hobson Richardson won the competition to design the new building. Born in 1838 at the Priestley Plantation in Saint James Parish, Louisiana, H.H. Richardson was the firstborn of Henry and Catherine Richardson. Henry Richardson had been born in Bermuda before emigrating to Boston and eventually settling in Louisiana. Henry became a successful merchant, operated a sugar plantation, and invested in real estate. In time, he married Catherine, the granddaughter of Joseph Priestley, whose father operated the nearby cotton plantation where H.H. was born.[10]

Catherine sold enslaved servants to cover their son's Harvard College tuition. Upon graduation, Richardson traveled abroad to study at École des Beaux-Arts (only the second American architect to do so), and he remained in Paris during the American Civil War. As with his undergraduate expenses, Richardson's parents financed his European education and travel from wealth derived from the unpaid labor of enslaved persons.[11]

Richardson met Phillips Brooks while studying at Harvard, and the Trinity project would center his schoolmate's preaching. Together, the pair imagined an inclusive environment that would boast good acoustics

---

9. Trinity Church, Boston. *Consecration*, 52–53.

10. Davis, Charles L. *Reading Richardson's Biography. Race and Architecture: Studying the Historical Instersections of Form and Culture.* April 4, 2014. Raceandarchitecture.com/2014/04/04/reading-richardsons-biography.

11. Blount, Howard. Louisiana Plantation Tours that Interpret the Slave Experience. Backroad Planet. Updated July 21, 2023. backroadplanet.com/louisiana-plantation-tours-slave experience.

and an uninterrupted view of the chancel and sanctuary. Perhaps seeded by Brooks' experience in Holy Trinity's auditorium-styled nave, this new building would declare God's magnificence through practical priorities: at Trinity, God's people of every station and situation could find a seat in a setting of heart-lifting beauty; God's people could hear clearly the Good News declared by the preacher and sung by the choir; and God's people could see the wonders prayed and celebrated before them.

With Trinity's move to the Back Bay, Brooks followed his parishioners who were leaving the Summer Street area and aimed for the many new neighbors he expected to attract. As common at the time (and would remain standard at Trinity until a 1952 act of the Massachusetts Legislature allowed for the practice's end), pew rentals were a necessary element of the congregation's financial stewardship.[12] Even so, Brooks also wanted as much gallery space as possible. Richardson designed the floor to seat 1,000, and, while the pew arrangement could make available different numbers of paid seats, Brooks insisted that the large galleries (seating approximately 400) remain free and open to all, with no solicitation. Brooks similarly inspired the parish's generosity, convincing the congregation that, in the spirit of welcome, if their pew was empty, their seat could be filled by anyone, at no charge.[13]

WELCOMING THE WORLD

In 1865 and 1866, Phillips Brooks first traveled to Europe and the Holy Land. During the Sabbatical sponsored by Holy Trinity, he wrote to his mother on October 2, 1865:

> To-day [I] have come into the region of Romish churches and relics. I have seen the skulls of the Three Wise Men, the thorns of Christ's Crown, the wood of the True Cross . . . and a church lined with the skulls and bones of the eleven thousand martyred virgins of Cologne. Of course you are expected to believe in them all, and isn't that pretty well for one day? But the [1248, Gothic] cathedral is very noble, by all means one of the great sights of the world.[14]

---

12. *Record of Special Meeting of Proprietors of Pews of Trinity Church in the City of Boston,* 1952.

13. Allen, *Life and Letters,* 658.

14. Brooks, *Letters of Travel,* 17.

In a second trip to Europe in 1870, Brooks traveled through Italy, Switzerland, and France. In the summer of 1872, he again adventured to Northern Europe. With Trinity's construction well underway in the summer of 1874, he returned to London before continuing to Venice.

Visiting hotels and museums, castles and churches, Brooks's travels rivaled Richardson's. The variety of architectural and artistic styles they encountered expanded the creative palette from which they conceived Trinity's features. For the exterior, the pair preferred neo-Romanesque fundamentals, and, like Philadelphia's Holy Trinity, they eschewed spiraling, Gothic flourishes for a structure of broader shoulders. Trinity's oddly shaped property abutted by streets, rather than other structures, meant its worship building and attached Parish House would be visible from all angles. With colors, patterns, and textures, Richardson carved catching, approachable beauty into its details on every side.

Richardson and Brooks also aimed Trinity's interior details to welcome the world and its many styles. To this end, Richardson selected John La Farge for the interior decoration. Though later best known for his stained-glass innovations, La Farge was an accomplished artist by the middle of the 1870s, having gained considerable acclaim as a painter, a grace he shared generously with Trinity's new church home.

The artist La Farge was born in New York in 1835. His father, Jean Frederic de la Farge, was a French emigre born in 1786. Napoleon Bonaparte sent Jean Frederic, only a teenager at the time, to Haitian Santo Domingo as part of a military operation to quell a rebellion among the island's enslaved people. Though de la Farge's troops suffered defeat, Haitian General Guerrier spared his life. The young Frenchman remained in Santo Domingo until learning of a plot by the enslaved to kill their oppressors on Easter Day 1806. De la Farge escaped to Europe and engaged in West Indies trade, which included involvement in transatlantic enslavement, as well as other business interests that benefitted from the unpaid labor of enslaved persons.[15, 16]

Upon his arrival in the United States, de la Farge invested in New York real estate and Louisiana plantations. He would anglicize his name to "Jean Frederick La Farge" in 1832, the same year he married Marie Louise Binsse de Saint-Victor. Of French descent, de Saint-Victor was born in New York in 1813, where her family settled after fleeing the Haitian Revolution. Her

---

15. McNickle, *Indian Man: A Life of Oliver La Farge*, 5–6.
16. Clarke, *Emigres in the Wilderness*, 165–78.

father, Louis Francois de Paul Binsse de Saint-Victor, had been one of the largest plantation owners on the island.[17]

John La Farge recalls in his memoir:

> I was just six years old, and I had wished to learn to draw and paint ... a mere boy's wish. My father took me to my grandfather, the father of my mother, who had for some time been a painter ... I never knew exactly how he came by his training ... My grandfather had been obliged to do something for himself, on coming to the United States with wife and children, and his escape from San Domingo and the ruin of his plantation and wealth, for his plantation was one of the largest in the islands or on the mainland ... His slaves, of course, were free and his plantation destroyed and his mansion and all about it turned into wilderness ... I remember my grandfather expressing a dislike to the institution of slavery. This came about through something he said, which I vaguely remember, of his having gone to the coast of Africa as a youngster, to get slaves; where he saw of course some of the horrors of what was to be the basis of his fortune.[18]

Brooks and Richardson chose decoration that complemented the architecture and contributed to an inviting whole. Though they provided La Farge notable freedom in his design, they presented the artist with at least two non-negotiables: the interior should be color-drenched in the European style, and the predominant color should be red. Richardson even specified the shade of red—*Pompeiian*, a vivid, orangey hue—which he intended to convey warmth and intimacy within the heavy walls, a space that could have been experienced as intimidating.[19]

La Farge led a team of young artists, including Augustus Saint-Gaudens and Francis Davis Millet, to produce one of American church architecture's most colorful, vibrant interiors. Working under tight time constraints, La Farge and his cohort achieved the dramatic decoration in just over four months.

Among the space's most prominent features, La Farge painted two large murals to flank the center-aisle entrance to the nave. Each image

---

17. Gouzi, Christine. "*The Emigration of French Artists in Europe After the Revolution of 1789.*" EHNE: Digital Encyclopedia of European History. Parish: Sorbonne University. Ehne.fr/enencyclopedia/themes/arts-in-europe/migration-and-artistic-identities/emigration-french-artists-in-europe-after-revolution-1789.

18. Cortissoz, *John La Farge: a Memoir*, 64–65.

19. Morgan, "From the Parish to the World," 6.

depicts a Christian Testament story: on the north wall, the story of the Samaritan woman who meets Jesus at the well, and on the south wall, the story of Nicodemus visiting Jesus at night. While La Farge determined the treatments, he chose the subjects in consultation with Brooks.

Just as Richardson's acoustics, clear lines of sight, and inviting galleries offer welcome, La Farge's paintings welcome Trinity's visitors with biblical images of *seekers* welcomed by Jesus—one born poor, an outcast in her society, and the other born wealthy, a privileged member of his community. In their setting, Brooks's and La Farge's decorations make clear that no matter one's status or circumstances, Trinty Church intends to offer the welcome of Christ to all.[20]

STORYTELLING IN GLASS

In his travels, Brooks became a devotee of stained glass, and he educated himself in its production and values. He furthered those studies during an 1877 sabbatical to England. While in Europe, Brooks visited several designers working on Trinity's memorial windows, most of which were commissioned and installed between 1877 and 1878. In a letter to vestryman Robert C. Winthrop, Brooks writes:

> My glass efforts in London have been very perplexing. Clayton and Bell were shamefully behindhand, and yet what they had done seemed to me even better than the window already in the Chancel. The Lord's Supper window is almost finished, and the centre window is just begun in glass from a cartoon which I like exceedingly. I have not definitely entrusted the other four windows to them, but I have no doubt that I shall do so this week.[21]

The original sacristy of Trinity Church features the window, *Ephphatha*. In 1884, Brooks himself gave the window (and its name) in thanksgiving for the parish's generosity, kindness, and support for his earlier sabbatical. Brooks conceived the design and engaged Burlison and Grylls of England in its execution.

The window depicts the encounter between Jesus and the man of Galilee who was "deaf and had an impediment in his speech."[22] At the left of the

---

20. Dukess, *Walls of Color Forum*.
21. Allen, *Life and Letters*, 2:227–28.
22. Mark 7:31–37 NRSV.

frame stands Jesus, his arm outstretched and his fingers nearly touching the lips of the one who has been brought to him. Around the pair stand Jesus's companions and the afflicted man's friends while a ship sails upon the Sea of Galilee in the background. Above the encounter, three angels bear a scroll.

At the bottom of the window, two smaller elements represent Jesus's baptism and the Last Supper. In the baptism scene, John, standing on the bank of the Jordan, pours water upon the head of Jesus, who stands in the river. In the Last Supper scene, Jesus breaks bread at the table with his disciples, John leaning upon his shoulder.[23] In all three representations in *Ephphatha*, Jesus has flowing, bright gold hair and a beard. In a letter to a friend, Brooks shares:

> I am glad you like the little window in the robing-room, because it was my own thought entirely and one in which I took the deepest interest. The makers did their work just as I wanted them to, and the result has already given me great satisfaction and inspiration. I hope that it will help a long line of the future Rectors of Trinity to speak with free and wise tongues.[24]

In the *Historical Sermon*, Brooks continues:

> There are few parishes where the hereditary chains are so many and so strong. To many and many a worshiper, this parish is dear because it is where his fathers worshiped. The names that stand on our pew roll today repeat, in a very large degree, the names of those whose good deeds stand thick along our records, and at whose entrance into the higher life our Church both sorrowed and rejoiced.[25]

Trinity's parishioners, including many among the most influential families in the city and nation, personally funded most of the new stained glass windows as memorials remembering their ancestors. Contributing households often chose scriptural images and scenes that they believed to reflect something about their loved ones' lives. Partnering with Brooks, families worked with artists to enliven those stories in glass. Some of these windows memorialize family members directly or indirectly involved in the trade of enslaved persons. Other windows depended upon the generosity of

---

23. Chester, *Trinity Church in the City of Boston*, 59–60.
24. Allen, *Phillips Brooks 1835–1893*, 289.
25. Trinity Church, Boston. *Consecration Services*, 52.

families whose wealth benefited from the unpaid labor of enslaved persons, both on southern plantations prior to the Civil War and, earlier, on Caribbean plantations.

Parishioner William Amory commissioned "Dorcas and the Good Samaritan" in memory of his parents, Thomas Coffin Amory and Hannah Rowe Linzee. Thomas had been a successful merchant from whom William Amory inherited great wealth. William significantly grew his inheritance and became a textile magnate, believed to have been a member of "The Boston Associates," which, by 1850, controlled most of New England's large cotton mills, monopolized the region's water-power sites, and manufactured textile machinery.

Stephen G. Deblois, who for many years served as Trinity's Treasurer and as a member of its Vestry, posthumously contributed the "Job and St. Stephen" window; its inscription reads: "In memory of the Deblois family of which many successive generations have served this church as Wardens and Vestrymen." The Deblois family were wealthy French Huguenots who emigrated to the colonies. In the late 1750s and early 1760s, newspaper advertisements describe items that Stephen's father, Gilbert Deblois, had for sale. These items included "tea, butter, cutlery... and a sloop of 70 tons, well fitted and suitable for the Guinea [slave] trade."[26] Other advertisements describe Gilbert and his brother, Lewis, acting as middlemen in the purchase and sale of enslaved persons. Over time, the Deblois family married into other successful merchant families, including the Amorys.[27]

Three grandsons of the Reverend John Sylvester John Gardiner, the Rector of Trinity Church from 1792–1830, completed contributions toward "The Last Supper," a chancel window dedicated to their grandfather. The grandsons—John Gardiner Cushing, Robert Maynard Cushing, and Thomas Forbes Cushing—were the sons of merchant John Perkins Cushing, who married Gardiner's only daughter, Mary Louisa. The Reverend Gardiner's father and grandfather enslaved people to serve their households, bought and sold enslaved persons, and invested in business ventures dependent upon the unpaid labor of enslaved people. Trinity records show that in 1781, John, "an adult negro servant of Sylvester Gardiner," was baptized, sponsored "by free negroes Lancaster Hill and his wife."[28]

---

26. Trinity Church, Boston, *Task Force for Justice and Reparations Report*, 16.

27. "To be sold by Gilbert Deblois," Advertisement. The Boston Gazette, November 9, 1761.

28. Oliver and Peabody, *The Records of Trinity Church, Boston, 1728–1830*, 595.

The Reverend Gardiner's father, John Gardiner, managed a sugar plantation in the West Indies while serving as British attorney general. Frank Wesley Pittman, referencing J.T. Hamilton's *History of the Moravians*, describes the elder Gardiner's conversion of enslaved people:

> In 1777, John Gardiner, a planter and solicitor of St. Christopher, invited Moravian missionaries from Antigua to come and instruct his slaves. He secured the approval of the governor and preaching began at Basseterre and at Palmetto Point, the estate of Gardiner. The converts were won by Gottwald and Schmeller; the latter visited about fifty plantations, and by the close of the eighteenth century, the number of Moravian Negroes in St. Christopher numbered more than two thousand.[29, 30]

ENCOUNTERING TRINITY'S HISTORY

At least two truths glimmer in Trinity's sanctuary and stone:

The Copley Square structure remains a breathtaking achievement, and, from conception to completion, the project expresses extraordinary faithfulness and skill. In 1885, the American Institute of Architects named Trinity the most important building in the United States, and Trinity is the only entry from the AIA's original list that continues to place in such rankings. Trinity's windows and murals have also sustained their status, not only in countless studies of the academy and the artistic schools they have influenced, but, fundamentally, in the stirring of souls. H.H. Richardson's richly textured exterior continues to invite visitors from every compass point. John La Farge's muraled interior still shares welcome with those who enter the nave. And Phillips Brooks's inspired leadership (to say nothing of his visage, featured many times over in wood, bronze, plaster, granite, and marble) still enlivens Trinity, the building's design and decoration fulfilling so many of his highest ideals and so much of his lofty ambition.

The scourges of slavery, racism, and privilege also stain the very grains of Trinity's mortar and glass. The development of Richardson's and La Farge's remarkable gifts depended upon their families' wealth, and their families' wealth depended upon enslaving and exploiting. Trinity's grand location and splendid scale depended upon the generosity of Trinity's foundational households, and many of those families' status depended upon

---

29. Pittman, *Slavery on the British West India Plantations*, 83.
30. Hamilton, *History of the Missions of the Moravian Church*, 64.

their antebellum interests in the textile and rum trades of the Deep South and Caribbean.

Despite their fine educations and extensive travels, Trinity's creators stood in the studios of William Morris, Clayton and Bell, Burlison and Grylls; leaned over ladders in Trinity's chancel and galleries; and, indeed, preached from Trinity's broadstep; and they depicted the characters of salvation history in their own, Western European image. While cultural syncretism has had a righteous place in Christian history, Trinity's creators lived in a multiracial and multicultural city, during a postbellum period forcefully challenging a monochromatic worldview. Likewise, while some admiring inheritors receive the legacy of Trinity's pictography like the patriarchal vocabulary of nineteenth-century letters, as an inevitable outcome of an era ignorant of its offenses, the worldliness of Brooks, Richardson, and their compatriots, and the care with which Trinity's creators undertook their work complicate any swift dispensation.

For all Brooks's well-meaning aspirations and for all the building accomplishes, Trinity prioritizes the welcome of its creators' communities: the white and the wealthy. While Trinity's beauty certainly functions iconically as a window to the Divine, the building also exists as a mirror for centuries of New England gentry and American nobility. For those the building prioritizes, this mirror offers a carnival reflection, one that hides their privilege from their view; one that conceals their benefits from institutionalized racism; one that hides their exclusivism in plain sight. Perhaps more dangerously, those the building prioritizes can co-opt Trinity's status to confirm their own supremacy, empowering and justifying their deliberate othering of outsiders, whether by race, origin, or class.

These two truths crackle with contradiction and challenge Trinity's heirs to reconcile an inheritance at once sublime and troubling.

ENDEAVORING TRINITY'S FUTURE

In Trinity's transepts, several tympanums (the half-moons created by the dome's buttressing) remain conspicuously unadorned. So, too, La Farge's main-tower prophets stare into un-muraled walls above the west pillars. In the *Historical Sermon*, Brooks charges the congregation to fill these spaces, to continue the holy work of enriching their worship home and their world:

> [Let us pray that Christ] may show Himself to us more and more completely as He really is; the rock under our feet and the limitless

air over our heads. O, let us pray that both may become more perfect to us in our new career, the rock more solid and the air more vast, the truths we hold more certain and more precious; the hope of more light on those truths, the watchfulness for deeper revelations of God, more vigilant and eager. Those be our prayers:—More strength; more light. More constancy; more progress.[31]

Brooks led his Boston parish to imagine a "progress" bearing their witness from a wooden meeting house, to an unremarkable Gothic structure, to a worship home that would excite architectural and artistic movements—and, then, *onward still*, to ever more glorious ministries of light and love. Formed by his experience and adventures, he cast a brazen vision, and, by dream, design, and decoration, he and his collaborators widened Trinity's welcome of the world. Yet, Brooks did not dare expect that the Copley Square building project fulfilled God's hopes for the world; he understood the faithful labor of widening must necessarily continue beyond his and his congregation's efforts. In the Historical Sermon, he writes:

> Let no soul go unsaved through any selfishness of ours. These galleries set free forever, and the assurance of what larger welcome may be needed and may be in our power to supply, bear witness that our Church accepts her responsibilities, and will try to speak the Gospel of the Lord she loves to all who will and hear.[32]

Brooks understood his call as a charge to advance God's reign in the time he had, with the people he served, in the city they lived. All who inherit Trinity's beauty and its burdens—parish and Church, village and state, nation and world—also receive Brooks's commission and prayer urging greater and greater faithfulness. Succeeding generations should aspire the bold trajectory Brooks set—not because he perfected it, but because he did not.

Celebrating all that is glorious and good in Trinity and her history, we labor to redeem whatever "selfishness" and blindness and cruelty we inherit. With the humility Brooks modeled, we share the wisdom our age has gleaned for renewal and not for judgment. He concludes the Historical Sermon:

> Friends, we must rise to thoughts beyond our fathers, or we are not our fathers' worthy children. Not to do in our days just what

---

31. Trinity Church, Boston, *Consecration Services*, 50.
32. Trinity Church, Boston, *Consecration Services*, 53.

our fathers did long ago, but to live as truly up to our light as our fathers lived up to theirs ... The Church has new standards, new ambitions, new ideas of work [, and] God help us to cast off every thing old and avoid every thing new which can keep our Church from doing perfectly that great work which we can hear our Lord calling her to do ...[33]

BIBLIOGRAPHY

Allen, Alexander V. G. *Life and Letters of Phillips Brooks.* Vol. 1. London: MacMillan, 1900.
———. *Life and Letters of Phillips Brooks.* Vol. 2. London: MacMillan, 1900.
———. *Phillips Brooks 1835–1893, Memories of His Life with Extracts from His Letters and Notebooks.* New York: Dutton, 1907.
Blount, Howard. *Louisiana Plantation Tours that Interpret the Slave Experience.* Backroad Planet. Updated July 21, 2023. backroadplanet.com/louisiana-plantation-tours-slave experience.
Brooks, Phillips. *Letters of Travel.* New York: Dutton, 1893.
Brown, Richard D., and Jack Tager. *Massachusetts: A Concise History.* Amherst: University of Massachusetts Press, 2000.
Chester, Arthur H. *Trinity Church in the City of Boston, an Historical and descriptive Account with a Guide to Its Windows and Paintings.* Cambridge: Wilson, 1888.
Clarke, T. Wood. *Emigres in the Wilderness.* New York: Friedman, 1967.
Cortissoz, Royal. *John La Farge: A Memoir and a Study.* Boston: Houghton Mifflin, 1911.
Dalzell, Robert F. *Enterprising Elite: The Boston Associates and the World They Made.* Cambridge: Harvard University Press, 1971.
Davis, Charles L. *Reading Richardson's Biography: Race and Architecture: Studying the Historical Instersections of Form and Culture.* April 4, 2014. Raceandarchitecture.com/2014/04/04/reading-richardsons-biography.
Dukess, Susan. "Walls of Color." A Forum at Trinity Church Boston, July 21, 2019. https://www.trinitychurchboston.org/blog/forum-walls-of-color.
Gouzi, Christine. "The Emigration of French Artists in Europe After the Revolution of 1789." EHNE: Digital Encyclopedia of European History. Parish: Sorbonne University. Ehne.fr/enencyclopedia/themes/arts-in-europe/migration-and-artistic-identities/emigration-french-artists-in-europe-after-revolution-1789.
Hamilton, J. Taylor. *History of the Missions of the Moravian Church During the Eighteenth and Nineteen Centuries.* Bethlehem: Times Publishing, 1900.
McNickle, D'Arcy. *Indian Man: A Life of Oliver La Farge.* Bloomington: Indiana University Press, 1971.
Morgan, Keith N. "From the Parish to the World: The Architectural Context of Trinity Church." In *The Makers of Trinity*, edited by James F. O'Gorman, 3–10. Boston: University of Massachusetts Press, 2004.
Paine, Thomas M. "Chairman of the Building Committee: Robert Treat Paine." In *The Makers of Trinity*, edited by James F. O'Gorman. Boston: University of Massachusetts Press, 2004.

---

33. Trinity Church, Boston. *Consecration Services,* 53.

Oliver, Andrew and James Bishop Peabody, eds. *The Records of Trinity Church, Boston, 1728–1830.* Boston: The Colonial Society of Massachusetts, 1982.

Pittman, Frank Wesley. *Slavery on the British West India Plantations in the Eighteenth Century.* Pennsylvania: Lancaster, 1926.

Record of Special Meeting of Proprietors of Pews of Trinity Church in the City of Boston, 1952.

"*To be sold by Gilbert Deblois.*" Advertisement. The Boston Gazette, November 9, 1761.

Trinity Church, Boston. *Consecration Services. February 9, 1877, with the Consecration Sermon by Rev. A. H. Vinton, D. D. an Historical Sermon by Rev. Phillips Brooks, and a Description of the Church Edifice by H. H. Richardson, Architect.* Boston: Printed by Order of the Vestry, 1877.

Trinity Church, Boston. *Task Force for Justice and Reparations Report.* Boston: Trinity Church, Boston, June 2022.

6

The Great Glad Tidings Tell
The Relevance of Phillips Brooks for Contemporary Preaching

RUTHANNA B. HOOKE

THE INFLUENCE OF PHILLIPS Brooks on the current theory and practice of preaching seems reducible to his definition of preaching as "the bringing of truth through personality."[1] This saying, which comes from Brooks's Lyman Beecher Lectures, given at Yale Divinity School in 1877 and published as *Eight Lectures on Preaching* in 1879, may be the only tidbit of Brooks's teachings on preaching that is generally known today. While Brooks's *Lectures on Preaching* are, in Gillis Harp's estimation, "one of the most broadly influential studies of preaching ever penned by an American," the *Lectures* themselves are not widely read and studied in the field of homiletics today.[2] However, the aphorism, "truth through personality," is preserved and continues to be quoted because it is a pithy articulation of the relationship of the person of the preacher to the truth of the message proclaimed, a subject that has been much discussed and debated in 20th century homiletical theory and practice. While Karl Barth argued vehemently that the personhood of the preacher was to be as little evident in preaching as possible, more recent homiletical theories have sought to carve out a more

---

1. Brooks, *Lectures on Preaching*, 5.
2. Harp, *Brahmin Prophet*, 116.

substantive place for the person of the preacher.[3] Such theories, though, often struggle with how to articulate this personal role without creating a model of preaching which allocates too much power or responsibility to the preacher, at the expense of the centrality of God's agency in preaching.

Into these debates Brooks's dictum has occasionally been drawn, but usually without reference to the fullness of his thought on preaching as it is found in the *Lectures on Preaching*. To read the *Lectures* themselves, however, is to discover a richness of reflection on preaching in general, and on the complex topic of the role of the personal in preaching in particular, that has much wisdom to offer to our current homiletical practices. Just as Ellen Wilbur, in compiling and editing *The Consolations of God: Great Sermons of Phillips Brooks*, was surprised at how vibrantly Brooks's sermons still speak to the contemporary reader, so too in reading *The Lectures on Preaching* I was impressed by the relevance of Brooks's teachings on preaching for contemporary preachers, especially concerning the way he expands on his description of preaching as "truth through personality" to articulate the role of the personal in preaching.[4] His teaching on preaching, as well as his preaching itself, demonstrates the truth of Peter Gomes's claim that Brooks "was always destined to be our contemporary."[5] In this essay I will explore Brooks's wisdom on preaching, as found in the *Lectures*, suggesting how his insights developed over time, and how they helped to account for his astonishing popularity during his lifetime. This wisdom, I will also argue, can be of great benefit for preachers today.

DEVELOPMENT OF BROOKS'S UNDERSTANDING OF THE PERSONAL IN PREACHING

It is intriguing that for a person who became arguably the most famous preacher of his time, Brooks's early preaching efforts were not successful. As Robert Flanagan recounts elsewhere in this volume, Brooks's first sermon at Sharon Chapel in Alexandria, Virginia, given while he was a second-year seminarian, received such a blank response from his hearers that Brooks, in dismay, climbed out a nearby window to escape the mortifying experience.[6]

---

3. For a brief introduction to Karl Barth's doctrine of preaching, and contemporary responses to it, see Long, *The Witness of Preaching*, 20–50.
4. Wilbur, *The Consolations of God*, xii.
5. Gomes, "Foreword," viii.
6. Flanagan, "In thy Dark Streets," *While Mortals Sleep*, 29.

Although in part he attributed these early setbacks to his sense that, as he wrote to his brother Frederick, "You know I was never much of a speaker,"[7] Brooks began to analyze his preaching failures as stemming from a lack of that very element of the personal that later became so central to his understanding of preaching. He later described his first sermon, possibly this sermon given at Sharon Chapel, in these disparaging terms: "I am sure that the sermon never was preached again. Its lack of simplicity and lack of Christ no doubt belonged together. It was probably an attempt to define doctrine instead of to show a man, a God, a Saviour."[8] The failure of this first sermon, according to Brooks, was due to the absence of reflection on the personal element of Christian faith, which is grounded in the very person of Christ.

While Brooks faults this sermon for lacking a focus on the person of Jesus Christ, the sermon apparently also lacked due attention to the personhood of those listening to him, since Brooks acknowledges the importance of improving this aspect of his preaching. He describes the evolution of his preaching at Sharon Chapel as developing "more and deeper sympathy with simple, honest men, and a clearer light into what common men's minds are doing, and how they may be taught to do better and nobler things."[9] He reflects on the crucial importance of paying attention to his hearers in a notebook entry from these seminary years:

> Until we have learned the universal language of human sympathy, how can we hope to speak so that all may hear us, and be drawn to us by what they hear? While we speak thus, each in the selfish tongue of our own interest or passions, our words will come sealed to the ears of our fellows, and all the consciousness that we are heard and understood by others, or the sweeter feeling that the world is better for our words, will all be lost.[10]

Brooks's seminary years were a time of learning the importance of sympathy with and understanding of hearers as essential to being an effective preacher. The value he placed on these dimensions of preaching was evident early in his ordained ministry, particularly in the eulogy he gave upon the death of Abraham Lincoln in 1865. In this sermon, which greatly enhanced Brooks's fame as a preacher, he extensively praises Lincoln's character,

---

7. Allen, *Life and Letters*, 1:290.
8. Brooks, "On the Pulpit and Popular Skepticism," 74.
9. Phillips Brooks to William G. Brooks, Jr., 6 Nov. 1858, quoted in Allen, *Life and Letters*, 1:88.
10. Allen, *Life and Letters*, 1:195.

describing the President as uniting head and heart into the wisdom that only truly simple people have. Lincoln, Brooks claims, had "genuine love for the people," and had "untired, undiscouraged faith in human nature."[11] These plaudits suggest that these were the very traits that Brooks himself aspired to in his developing preaching ministry—the wisdom that emerges from the joining of head and heart, an optimistic faith in human nature, and an authentic love for people.

THE PERSON WHO PREACHES THE PERSONAL CHRIST

By the time Brooks delivered the *Lectures on Preaching* his insights into the importance of the personal in preaching had become fully developed. As his earlier thoughts on this topic suggest, Brooks argues in the *Lectures* that there are three "persons," or dimensions of the personal, that are of crucial importance in preaching. The first of these is the person of Christ; having learned from the flaws of his first sermon, which "attempt[ed] to define doctrine instead of to show a man, a God, a Saviour,"[12] Brooks insists that Christian faith is based on a person, and hence must be communicated personally:

> However the Gospel may be capable of statement in dogmatic form, its truest statement we know is not in dogma but in personal life. Christianity is Christ; and we can easily understand how a truth which is of such peculiar character that a person can stand forth and say of it, "I am the Truth," must always be best conveyed through, must indeed be almost incapable of being perfectly conveyed except through personality.[13]

The centrality of Christ leads inevitably to the centrality of the personhood and personal involvement of the preacher in preaching, and this personality is always oriented toward and open to the third "person" involved in the sermon, which is the hearer. These three elements of preaching interweave continually in the *Lectures on Preaching*, indicating how inseparable they were for Brooks.

As various analyses of Brooks have noted, his Christology is centered on the Incarnation, the miracle of God dwelling with us, which he describes

---

11. Brooks, "Sermon on the Death of Abraham Lincoln," in *20 Centuries of Great Preaching*, 130.

12. Brooks, "On the Pulpit and Popular Skepticism," 74.

13. Brooks, *Lectures on Preaching*, 7.

so poignantly in his hymn, "O Little Town of Bethlehem": "O come to us, abide with us, our Lord, Emmanuel." The Incarnation sums up for Brooks the closeness of God to each human life, which is a frequent theme of his sermons.[14] In "The Nearness of God," for instance, Brooks describes Paul's speech to the Athenians on the unknown God as conveying this message:

> You are restless, always on the brink of something you never reach. . . .Behold, I tell you what it means. It is God with you. It is Emmanuel. His presence it is that will not let you be at peace. You do not see Him, but He is close by you. You will never be at peace until you do see Him and come to Him to find the peace which He will not let you find away from Him. Come unto me, and I will give you rest." That was the revelation of the Incarnation.[15]

It was this Christ that Brooks felt compelled to preach and, in his *Lectures on Preaching*, exhorts preachers to preach, especially in an age which, in Brooks's estimation, was rife with fatalism and helplessness. As Brooks maintains, "there never was an age that so needed to have Christ preached to it, the personal Christ. In his personality the bewildered soul must re-find its own personal life."[16] The personhood of Christ is necessary for the salvation of the persons among whom he became incarnate.

In order for the personal Christ to reach the persons for whom he came, the personality of the preacher is indispensable. It is in describing the meaning of this requirement that Brooks offers some of his most trenchant and lastingly valuable insights. The word "personality" may be a stumbling block for some contemporary readers, as it smacks of ego and drawing attention to oneself; however, what Brooks means by "truth through personality" is that Christian proclamation needs to be truly integrated into and expressive of the life of the preacher:

> The truth must come really through the person, not merely over his lips, not merely into his understanding and out through his pen. It must come through his character, his affections, his whole intellectual and moral being. It must come genuinely through him. I think that, granting equal intelligence and study, here is the great difference which we feel between two preachers of the Word. The Gospel has come *over* one of them and reaches us tinged and flavoured with his superficial characteristics, belittled with his

---

14. Slocum, *The Anglican Imagination*, 92.
15. Brooks, "The Nearness of God," 99.
16. Brooks, *Lectures on Preaching*, 224.

littleness. The Gospel has come *through* the other, and we receive it impressed and winged with all the earnestness and strength that there is in him. In the first case the man has been but a printing machine or a trumpet. In the other case he has been a true man and a real messenger of God.[17]

This description of "truth through personality" articulates the relationship between the two with subtlety and wisdom; for "personality" to be involved in preaching does not mean drawing attention to oneself in a shallow way; rather, it means allowing the Gospel to permeate one's being entirely.

Throughout the *Lectures on Preaching* Brooks delves into what it means for the Gospel to "come *through*" the preacher. Brooks argues that this personal involvement in preaching ought to shape the preacher's ministry from its inception, influencing the pastor's education so that it is not "the mere training to certain tricks," nor is it "the furnishing with abundant knowledge," but is rather "the kneading and tempering of a man's whole nature till it becomes of such a consistency and quality as to be capable of transmission."[18] This description of theological education prefigures much of the recent scholarship on the nature of such education, which emphasizes, like Brooks, that theological education is not merely the learning of techniques nor the acquisition of knowledge, but must be formation of the whole person.[19]

As preachers are being formed, and throughout their ministries, the necessity of the personal dimension in preaching means that preachers must find their own voice and not copy that of others: "if your ministry is to be good for anything, it must be your ministry, and not a feeble echo of any other man's."[20] Brooks acknowledges that the risk of imitation in preaching is considerable precisely because of the personal dimension of it; because the personal skill of the preacher is so evident in great preaching, others

---

17. Brooks, *Lectures on Preaching*, 8; emphasis Brooks's. As a person of his time, Brooks exclusively refers to the preacher using male pronouns. In an attempt to counteract Brooks's assumption that the preacher is male, in this essay I have used female pronouns to refer to the preacher. I hope that this disjunction between Brooks's language and my own will remind readers that preaching was practiced by people of various genders in Brooks's time, as it is in ours.

18. Brooks, *Lectures on Preaching*, 9.

19. For recent discussions on theological education as wholistic intellectual, personal, and embodied formation, see, for instance, Bass and Dykstra, eds., *For Life Abundant*; and Barreto, ed., *Thinking Theologically*; and Smith, *The End of Theological Education*.

20. Brooks, *Lectures on Preaching*, 106.

want to imitate this preacher's personal style. Although Brooks does not state this directly, one assumes that he is well aware that he himself, as one of the foremost preachers of the day, is being too often imitated, to deleterious effect. He points out that to avoid imitation, one cannot simply resolve not to do it, for often it happens unconsciously. Rather, the only antidote to imitating another preacher is that "you must bring a real self of your own to meet this intrusive self of another man that is crowding in upon you."[21] One implication of this criterion for preaching is that preachers must at all times be honest in what they proclaim: "Never dare to say in the pulpit or in private, through ardent excitement or conformity to what you know you are expected to say, one word, which at the moment you say it, you do not believe."[22]

As a teacher of homiletics, I find these directives of enormous value for preachers. Entering into the vital and often intimidating task of proclamation, preachers too often tend to copy another person's style or content, rather than seeking that which is their own. Likewise, they are often tempted simply to parrot the doctrine they have been taught, or what they are expected to say, rather than to preach what they themselves believe and know to be true. As Brooks notes, "The deep sense of the solemnity of the minister's work has often a tendency to repress the free individuality of the preacher."[23] The only remedy for this repression, which can lead to dishonesty in preaching, is to "bring a real self of [one]s own" into the task of preaching. Indeed, one of the dangers of advice in homiletics that urges preachers to "get out of the way," or to make their own personhood invisible in preaching, is that it leads to imitation of others or to the proclaiming of words that the preacher does not herself believe. Hence, as Brooks notes, the remedy for these distortions of preaching must be the preacher's appropriate valuing of and engagement with her own personhood and voice.

The risk of such counsel, however, is that it can lead to the preacher's foregrounding her personhood or "personality" in a shallow or egocentric way. Brooks offers direction on how to counteract this danger, insisting that preachers need to bring their personalities to bear in preaching not in a trivial but in a profound way:

> Be yourself by all means, but let that good result come not by cultivating merely superficial peculiarities and oddities. Let it be by

21. Brooks, *Lectures on Preaching*, 169.
22. Brooks, *Lectures on Preaching*, 107.
23. Brooks, *Lectures on Preaching*, 23.

winning a true self full of your own faith and your own love. The deep originality is noble, but the superficial originality is miserable. It is so easy to be a John the Baptist, so far as the desert and the camel's hair and locusts and wild honey go. But the devoted heart to speak from, and the fiery words to speak, are other things.[24]

To bring one's personality to preaching does not mean to develop superficial stylistic idiosyncrasies, nor to clothe preaching in the trappings of ego, but rather to bring the fullness of one's own faith and love.

Brooks cautions against the intrusion of ego into the sermon also by warning preachers not to dwell on their own personal story, "the autobiographical style of preaching" that is "the crudest attempt to blend personality and truth."[25] Not only does such preaching become oppressive and tiresome over time, but it narrows the range of the congregation's experience of God to that which the preacher himself has experienced. Instead of such "crude" importations of the preacher's personal experience into the sermon, a preacher should be "always holding back the mere envelope of accident and circumstance in which the truth has embodied itself to him, and yet sending forth the truth with all the clearness and force which it has gathered from him from that embodiment."[26] This description of how a preacher's personal experience figures in a sermon, as the source of the "clearness and force" of the truth proclaimed, rather than itself becoming the content of the sermon, is a subtle and wise way to describe this complex relationship between personal experience and the sermon itself. Often preachers make the mistake of believing that the only way to demonstrate a personal stake in a sermon is to employ personal stories. While occasionally such personal disclosures are illuminating of the Gospel message, it is also sometimes the case that such stories are intrusive in the sermon. Often a better approach is the one Brooks describes, of allowing these personal experiences to give the sermon its "clearness and force," the hidden source of the sermon's passion that need not be directly relayed.

An unhealthy involvement of the ego in preaching can also appear in the preacher's self-doubts, her questions about whether her sermons are "good" or not. Brooks firmly states that such thoughts are devastating for preachers: "No man ever yet thought whether he was preaching well

---

24. Brooks, *Lectures on Preaching*, 24.
25. Brooks, *Lectures on Preaching*, 116–17.
26. Brooks, *Lectures on Preaching*, 120.

without weakening his sermon."[27] Similarly, the preacher's desire to preach a "great" sermon is "fatal" for preachers.[28] Both the desire to be popular as a preacher, and that popularity itself, is damaging for preachers. After naming this focus on the self and its performance that is so crippling to preachers, Brooks describes, with his characteristically image-rich language, the moment when this self-consciousness falls away:

> I think there are few higher or more delightful moments in a preacher's life than that which comes sometimes when, standing before a congregation and haunted by questionings about the merit of your preaching, which you hate but cannot drive away, at last, suddenly or gradually, you find yourself taken into the power of your truth, absorbed in one sole desire to send it into the men whom you are preaching to; and then every sail is set, and your sermon goes bravely out to sea, leaving yourself high and dry upon the beach, where it has been holding your sermon stranded.[29]

This description captures vividly a dynamic of preaching that probably every preacher has experienced: the self-critique that can run like a debilitating commentary underneath every word one preaches, and then, conversely, the bliss that comes when this undermining voice is left behind and the preacher is simply one with the Word she is proclaiming. Brooks's awareness of this dynamic, and skillful description of it, points to his sensitivity in diagnosing the machinations of the human mind, and in recognizing the movement of God which transcends and transforms these patterns of thought. Both the sense that one's sermons are successful, and being told by others that they are so, and, conversely, the conviction that one's sermons are failures, are damaging to preachers, and are a distortion of the personal engagement in preaching which Brooks commends. Rather, the preacher's sole focus ought to be on "God's truth and men's salvation."[30]

THE PERSONS WHO HEAR

It is through the personality of the preacher that the truth of the personal Christ is conveyed to the third "person" Brooks has always in mind in the *Lectures on Preaching*: the person who hears the sermon. Describing the

27. Brooks, *Lectures on Preaching*, 51.
28. Brooks, *Lectures on Preaching*, 150.
29. Brooks, *Lectures on Preaching*, 52.
30. Brooks, *Lectures on Preaching*, 212.

relationship among these three persons, Brooks states that Christian ministry, "is not the mere practice of a set of rules and precedents, but is a broad, free, fresh meeting of a man with men, in such close contact that the Christ who has entered into his life may, through him, enter into theirs."[31] Through the encounter of one human being with another, the person of Christ becomes manifest and can be appropriated. Thus, the preacher must be attentive to both persons in this relationship, to God and to the hearers. It is through the openness of the preacher's life "on both sides, towards the truth of God and towards the needs of men" that the personal encounter between Christ and the hearer can take place.[32]

The openness of the preacher toward her people has fundamentally to do with knowing and loving them. Brooks urges preachers to stay in one congregation for a long time, to get to know the congregants thoroughly, and to develop the capacity to discern what they need to hear. Their needs ought to govern the content of sermons, more than the preacher's inclination or her plan for the trajectory of her sermons over time: "first comes the sympathetic and wise perception of what the people need." This perception is not the result of a brief contact with parishioners, but rather is "the aggregate effect of a large sympathetic intercourse; the fruit of a true knowledge of human nature, combined with a special knowledge of these special people, and cordial interest in the conditions under which they live."[33] In sum, to preach what her people need to hear, the preacher must cultivate "an alert mind, fully interested in the times in which it lives, and a devout soul really loving the souls with which it has to deal."[34] Above all, to preach well the preacher must love those to whom she preaches, and must care about them more than she does about the quality of her sermon in itself.

To love and to be open to one's hearers means, above all, respecting them. The preacher's power stems in great measure from the "genuine respect for the people whom he preaches to," and Brooks maintains that this respect is rare. Preachers may feel sympathy of sentiment or liking for their congregants, or they may seek their cooperation, or may patronize them, "but of a real profound respect for the men and women whom we preach to, simply as men and women, of a deep value for the capacity that is in them, a

---

31. Brooks, *Lectures on Preaching*, 106.
32. Brooks, *Lectures on Preaching*, 26.
33. Brooks, *Lectures on Preaching*, 154.
34. Brooks, *Lectures on Preaching*, 154.

sense that we are theirs and not they ours, I think that there is far too little."[35] To respect hearers truly is to value their souls, and Brooks insists that feeling the value of human souls is the "power which lies at the center of all success in preaching."[36] The last of Brooks's *Lectures on Preaching* is devoted to this topic; he states that he has saved the most important topic for last, holding that valuing human souls is the power that fuels all great preaching, makes up for many deficits in a preacher's skills, and, if absent, cannot be compensated for by any other capacities the preacher may have. Among all of the other abilities of the preacher, to be able to feel the worth of the human souls to whom one preachers is the one indispensable capacity. Only this perception can make sense of the wonders that God has done for us, making these gifts credible to the preacher herself as well as to hearers:

> You must discern in all these men and women some inherent preciousness for which even the marvel of the Incarnation and the agony of Calvary was not too great, or it is impossible that you should keep your faith in those stupendous truths which Bethlehem and Calvary offer to us. Some source of fire from which these dimmed sparks come, some possible renewal of the fire that is in them still, some sight of the education through which each soul is passing, and some suggestion of the special personal perfection to which each may attain, all this must brighten before you, as you look at them; and then the truths of your theology shall not be thrown into confusion nor faded into unreality by your ministry to men.[37]

The true driving force of all good preaching is the perception that the people to whom one preaches are worthy of God's dwelling with them and dying for them, and that these people have before them a destiny that is glorious, toward which the preacher aims to draw them.

Brooks's insistence on the value of the human soul, both in his sermons and in his *Lectures on Preaching*, stems from the centrality of the Incarnation in his thought. As Gillis Harp notes, for Brooks "the condescension of God in the Incarnation was not chiefly a sign of God's gracious mercy (though it was certainly that) but, above all, it was the most eloquent divine affirmation of human worth."[38] This conviction led Brooks to insist on the

---

35. Brooks, *Lectures on Preaching*, 53.
36. Brooks, *Lectures on Preaching*, 255.
37. Brooks, *Lectures on Preaching*, 261.
38. Harp, *Brahmin Prophet*, 175.

inherent nobility of the human person, causing some of his contemporaries to complain that he lacked an adequate sense of the sinfulness of human nature.[39] While it is true that Brooks does not dwell on human depravity in his sermons, he is deeply concerned with the form of human sin consisting of human failure to grasp their essential worthiness, that in them which made Christ willing to die to save them. This failure leads people to lead shallow lives, ignorant of God and of God's purposes for them. One of the repeated themes in Brooks's sermons is his concern for the shallowness of people's lives. He notes that "the great mass of people are stunted and starved with superficialness...They never touch the real reasons and meanings of living."[40] Such people are afraid to have anything to do with God, and they turn away from God.

Given this form of human sin, a central task of preaching is to help hearers perceive and claim their own worthiness and thus live in the larger life that God desires for them. Perceiving the value of those to whom she preaches, the task of the preacher is to inspire in them that same sense of their value, which means to rescue them from the littleness of their lives to the largeness of their life in Christ: "we must bring men's life up to Him and not bring Him down to men's life."[41] The preacher must counter the human impulse to live superficial and small lives by helping people to see their glorious potential and making them want to strive toward this ideal. In this effort the preacher will often need to give people what they *need* more than what they *want*; understanding the value of humans will motivate the preacher's courage to speak the truth the people must hear in order to claim their true potential.

To proclaim the worth of the human soul is not only a necessity but is, for Brooks, a source of joy in preaching. He describes "this value of the human soul for its own sake, as constituting the constant reserve of pleasure in the ministry."[42] While other sources of joy in ministry depend to some extent on circumstances, "the mere pleasure of dealing with man as man, as a being valuable in himself, for this no peculiar happiness of circumstances is needed."[43] The mere presence of those with whom one ministers is a constant source of delight from which the preacher can draw. The delight

---

39. Harp, *Brahmin Prophet*, 179.
40. Brooks, "The Seriousness of Life," 108.
41. Brooks, *Lectures on Preaching*, 81.
42. Brooks, *Lectures on Preaching*, 263.
43. Brooks, *Lectures fon Preaching*, 263.

the preacher derives from her the parishioners is but one of the ways that they minister to her, and indeed, says Brooks:

> This ministry of the people to the preacher. . .is often greater than any ministry that the preacher can render to the people. I assure you that the relation between the pastor and his parish is not right if the pastor thinks the obligation to be all on one side, if while he lives with them. . .he is not always full of gratitude for what they have done for him. A pastor who is insensible to this cannot do the best good to his people.[44]

The combination of gratitude for one's hearers, delight in working with them, and conviction that their souls have value strongly motivated Brooks's preaching, along with his passionate desire to share the truth of Jesus Christ with them.

SOURCES OF BROOKS'S POPULARITY

Gillis Harp argues that Brooks's enormous popularity was due to his keen understanding of the time in which he lived, and thus his popularity sheds light on the religious thought and tenor of that time. Brooks was acclaimed, Harp maintains, because he grasped the spirit of the time and spoke to it convincingly. Harp describes Brooks as seeking to modernize the Christian faith, both theologically and culturally. In light of Darwinism and the development of historical criticism of the Bible, Brooks tended to emphasize religious experience and ethical responsibility more than a deep exploration of Christian doctrine. Harp argues that Brooks was deeply influenced by the Romanticism of Ralph Waldo Emerson and others, with its emphasis on feeling and on existential experience of God more than dogma.[45] Likewise, Brooks did not engage in detailed scriptural exegesis, but tended to draw a single principle from the text and then expound on that principle in more general terms. His preaching style was literary and imaginative rather than didactic. All of this, Harp maintains, made Brooks enormously successful in making Christianity appealing to his hearers, as he made Christianity accessible and palatable to a modern audience that could no longer accept Christian doctrine in its fullness at face value.

---

44. Brooks, *Lectures on Preaching*, 273–74.
45. Harp, *Brahmin Prophet*, 115.

While these aspects of Brooks's preaching may partly account for his popularity, I propose that it was also in large part his sensitive and wise understanding of the personal in preaching that made him so compelling as a preacher in a time when religious belief was challenged by modernity. Brooks himself understood his effectiveness in this way. He maintains that the general principle of "truth through personality" is more essential than ever in times when religious belief is waning. In response to the irreligious nature of his time, the preacher nevertheless perceives that underneath this secularity is a deep religious impulse, and he preaches to that impulse. However, he can only do so effectively if he is himself grounded in his faith:

> But the main thing is to know our own ground as spiritual men, and stand on its assured and tested strength. And that strength can be tested only by our own experience; and so once more we come round to our old first truth, that the man is behind the ministry, that what is in the sermon must be in the preacher first.[46]

Brooks acknowledges that preachers have lost social standing in his time, but he maintains that this is a development to be celebrated rather than lamented, for this loss of status means that preachers must be valued only for who they are, for their personal faith and conviction. In a time of skepticism, the preacher's way of convincing unbelievers "must be in his own manhood, in his character, in his being such a man, and so apprehending truth himself, that truth through him can come to other men."[47] In addition to the personal involvement of the preacher, the strength of preaching rests on the truth that is being communicated, the truth of the personal Christ, rather than on the office of preacher as such. The preacher who accepts the loss of the status of the preaching office "preaches truth and duty on their own intrinsic authority, and wins personal power and influence because he does not seek them, but seeks the prevalence of righteousness and the salvation of men's souls."[48]

In addition to the personhood of the preacher, and the truth of the personal Christ that is preached, Brooks's genuine respect for the person of the hearer was another key to his effectiveness as preacher in the modern age. As Brooks describes it: "The minister who succeeds is the minister who in the midst of a sordid age trusts the heart of man who is the child of God,

---

46. Brooks, *Lectures on Preaching*, 230.

47. Brooks, "Pulpit and Popular Skepticism," 298; quoted in Harp, *Brahmin Prophet*, 172.

48. Brooks, *Lectures on Preaching*, 249.

and knows that it is not all sordid, and boldly speaks to it of God his Father as though he expected it to answer. And it does answer." Other ministers, who do not trust this goodness in the hearer, and who preach with limited expectations, are astounded by the success of the pastor who preaches to the higher side of a person.[49] This description points not only to a general rule regarding preaching, but also suggests how Brooks understood his own effectiveness and popularity, despite the challenges of preaching in his time: he valued his hearers, cared about them, and sought to draw them toward the highest ideals which they themselves wished to attain.

Brooks offers an account of a possibly fictional dialogue between a pastor and a hearer that suggests his understanding of how his words touch the religious skeptic:

> I am not convinced by what you say. I am not sure that I cannot answer every one of your arguments," said a man with whom a preacher had been pleading, "but one thing which I confess I cannot understand. It puzzles me, and makes me feel a power in what you say. It is why you should care enough for me to take all this trouble, and to labour with me as if you cared for my soul." It is a power which every man must feel."[50]

Brooks here articulates an intuition that it was this care for the human soul that touched people, even those who, in his skeptical age, were otherwise inclined to doubt the truths of the faith.

It was this combination of love for his hearers and conviction of the truths of the Christian faith that led Brooks to insist that all preachers ought to delight in their calling, for there is no other joy on earth greater than "the glorifying of the Lord and the saving of the souls of men."[51] Brooks chides preachers who, daunted by the challenges of preaching in modernity, complain about their vocation "as if it were full of hardships and disappointments," when it ought to be a source of profound joy. He recounts one such experience, when the awesome gift of preaching was borne in upon him:

> I always remember one special afternoon, years ago, when the light faded from the room where I was preaching and the faces melted together into a unit as of one impressive pleading man, and I felt them listening though I could hardly see them; I remember this accidental day as one of the times when the sense of the

---

49. Brooks, *Lectures on Preaching*, 242.
50. Brooks, *Lectures on Preaching*, 257.
51. Brooks, *Lectures on Preaching*, 82.

privilege of having to do with people as their preacher came out almost overpoweringly.[52]

It is evident in Brooks's writings about preaching, and in descriptions such as this, that he deeply felt the responsibility and the joy of preaching, motivated as it was by love of God and love of people.

Such evocations of Brook's experience of preaching also suggest that the catharsis that took place in his preaching had to do as much with the affect he produced in his hearers as it did with his words. The capacity to produce that affect, and thus to preach effectively to his time was itself rooted in Brooks's threefold love—of God, of hearers, and of preaching itself. He seems to have perceived what people most deeply needed to hear in his time, which was that they were valued enough in God's eyes that Christ died for them. Despite their skepticism about aspects of Christian doctrine, this message resonated and won them over in large numbers. Moreover, the message itself resonated because it was authentic to Brooks himself; his love for his hearers was genuine, and they could sense it. Furthermore, that love was rooted in Brooks's personal knowledge of God, and in his understanding of how his own personhood figured in the sermon in such a way that the message of the Gospel could be conveyed through him. In sum, Brooks preached effectively to his time because of his care for his hearers, his love of Christ, his delight in preaching itself, and his own self-knowledge. These were the fuel of a preaching career that captivated his hearers and made Brooks the preaching phenomenon that he was.

CONCLUSION: BROOKS AS OUR CONTEMPORARY

Although Brooks was a sensational preacher in his own day, it could be argued that his preaching style and philosophy ought not to be emulated by preachers today. Gillis Harp maintains as much, arguing that Brooks's popularity was not an unqualified blessing for future Protestant mainline preachers. Harp suggests that, by retaining the style and fervor of evangelicalism, while moving away from an emphasis on dogma and rigorous attention to Scripture, Brooks's preaching had the effect of diminishing the traditional authority of the Christian faith. While Brooks himself, through his personal skill as a preacher, could make a modernized Christian faith palatable to the listener, those without his gifts could not maintain this

---

52. Brooks, *Lectures on Preaching*, 83–84.

synthesis, leading to a waning of the authority of the Protestant mainline pulpit.[53] Moreover, Brooks's emphasis on "personality" has led to a deleterious focus on the person of the preacher.[54] These critiques suggest that Brooks ought not to be a model for contemporary preachers.

However, a closer look at Brooks's own theology and theory of preaching suggests some of the deeper roots of his popularity in his own time, as well as how his wisdom on preaching can speak to our own time. Brooks's wisdom suggests that what drew listeners to him was not principally his rhetorical skill or his abstracting from dogma and Scripture, but rather his profound understanding of what preaching itself is, and how the preacher needs to enter into it. His description of preaching as "the bringing of truth through personality," when unpacked, rather than leading toward an enhancement of the preacher's ego and hence a distortion of preaching, directs preachers toward a subtle and wise balancing of the person of Christ, the person of the hearer, and the person of the preacher. Brooks writes sensitively about the appropriate role of the preacher's personhood—the necessity of conviction, authenticity, and honesty, and a rejection of imitation; the stripping away of the ego, and a refusal to dwell on external voices of validation or criticism; and deep personal experience of God which fuels the sermon but need not be directly named. Balancing this insight into the preacher's personal involvement in preaching is the preacher's attitude toward the hearer: genuine respect for the human soul and calling it to its true potential; a love and delight in hearers; and a gratitude for the gifts they give the preacher. Incorporating these insights can guide and empower contemporary preachers, as well as those in Brooks's time.

In our time, guidance on preaching abounds, but it often takes the form of "how-to" resources. As valuable as these are, it is crucial for preachers to reflect on the deeper sources of their preaching, the subtler temptations, and the true privilege that preaching is. This is particularly true in our own time, when, even more than in Brooks's era, it can be easy for preachers to despair of the value of their calling. Preachers today regularly complain of the "hardships and disappointments" of their vocation. People are turning away from Christianity in greater numbers than they did in Brooks's day. Nevertheless, the task of preaching, to glorify God and save human souls, is as valuable and important in our time as it ever has been. In the face of the challenges facing contemporary preachers, and the vital importance of

---

53. Harp, *Brahmin Prophet*, 128, 207.
54. Harp, *Brahmin Prophet*, 214.

their calling, Brooks's insights on what makes preaching effective deserve a fresh hearing, for they are still relevant in our time, perhaps even more so than they were in his. For preachers questioning the efficacy of their work or seeking to better understand their role in this mysterious occupation, Brooks is a mentor offering rare wisdom, subtlety, and enthusiasm for the preaching task. His voice is of great value for preachers who want to think more deeply about their preaching or to rediscover the passion and joy that Brooks himself brought to preaching, and that his writings make available to us today.

BIBLIOGRAPHY

Allen, Alexander V. G. *Life and Letters of Phillips Brooks*, 2 vols. New York: Dutton, 1900.
Barreto, Eric D., ed. *Thinking Theologically: Foundations for Learning*. Minneapolis: Fortress, 2015.
Bass, Dorothy C. and Craig Dykstra, eds. *For Life Abundant: Practical Theology, Theological Education, and Christian Ministry*. Grand Rapids: Eerdmans, 2008.
Brooks, Phillips. *Eight Lectures on Preaching*. London: SPCK, 1959.
———. "The Nearness of God." In *The Consolations of God: Great Sermons of Phillips Brooks*, edited by Ellen Wilbur, 94–106. Grand Rapids: Eerdmans, 2003.
———. "On the Pulpit and Popular Skepticism." In *Essays and Addresses*, 295–310. Princeton: Princeton Review, March 1879.
———. "Sermon on the Death of Abraham Lincoln." In *20 Centuries of Great Preaching*, vol. 6, edited by Clyde E. Fant Jr. and William M. Pinson Jr., 125–35. Waco, TX: Word, 1971.
———. "The Seriousness of Life." In *The Consolations of God: Great Sermons of Phillips Brooks*, edited by Ellen Wilbur, 107–17. Grand Rapids: Eerdmans, 2003.
Flanagan, Robert D. "In thy Dark Streets: The Seminary Experience of Phillips Brooks, 1856–1859." In *While Mortals Sleep: Reading Phillips Brooks Through Twnety-First-Century Eyes*, edited by Robert D. Flanagan, 16–35. Eugene: Wipf and Stock, 2025.
Gomes, Peter J. "Foreword." In *The Consolations of God: Great Sermons of Phillips Brooks*, edited by Ellen Wilbur, xiii–xi. Grand Rapids: Eerdmans, 2003.
Harp, Gillis J. *Brahmin Prophet: Phillips Brooks and the Path of Liberal Protestantism*. Lanham, MD: Rowman & Littlefield, 2003.
Long, Thomas G. *The Witness of Preaching*. 3rd ed. Louisville: Westminster John Knox, 2016.
Slocum, Robert Boak. *The Anglican Imagination: Portraits and Sketches of Modern Anglican Theologians*. Farnham, UK: Ashgate, 2015.
Smith, Ted. A. *The End of Theological Education*. Grand Rapids: Eerdmans, 2023.
Wilbur, Ellen, ed. *The Consolations of God: Great Sermons of Phillips Brooks*. Grand Rapids: Eerdmans, 2003.

7

Abide With Us
Brooks's Rise to the Bishop of Massachusetts

Robert D. Flanagan

PHILLIPS BROOKS WAS DESTINED for greatness. His years in Philadelphia were a proving ground during which Brooks gained practical skills as a pastor, teacher, priest, and preacher. He was no longer a student hoping to do some good after he was ordained. When Brooks returned to Boston in 1869, Brooks had become an Episcopal Church rising star and a person of growing notoriety. Phillips was becoming the muscular, manly Christian he wanted to be by serving Christ through the mechanisms of his denomination in service of the country and beyond.

PHILLIPS BROOKS RISES TO PROMINENCE

The announcement about his Boston return formerly introduced him to the nation. In 1869, the New York Times (The Times) described him: "Rev. Phillip[s] Brooks, one of the most eloquent pulpit orators this country has produced, has resigned his charge in Philadelphia and accepted the invitation of Trinity Church in the City of Boston, to become its rector."[1] The

---

1. The primary source material for this chapter is *The New York Times*. With its distance from Boston and Philadelphia, the newspaper filters out much of the idolization and idealized view of Brooks. The New York Times reporting is more sober and presents Brooks's positive and negative character traits.

thirty-three-year-old Boston native was returning home to lead one of the nation's most prominent churches. After successfully leading two Philadelphia churches and reaching that city's ecclesiastical pinnacle, Phillips began the climb that solidified his national prominence.

Brooks's climb took time. Not until he preached at the Church of the Incarnation, Manhattan, where his brother Arthur was rector, on Sunday, April 20, 1879, did The Times report at length on Brooks.[2] The sermon's dry and intellectual topic was "evolution not atheism," and yet, "a tremendous crush"[3] gathered to hear it. The article explained Brooks's discussion of God's economy, turning to humanity's inclusion, "It is true that no circumstances can make a great man out of little, but it is true also that the lives of thousands of patient men contribute; not one is wasted."[4] Thus, humans of every race and creed are valued by God. Brooks's sermon then turned to knowledge. In that discourse, he stated, "Men say that the system of religious truths is changing. Certainly, it is. Thank God for it!"[5] He continued, "We hold fast to the old Church and the old faith, but we have no feeling that the Church holds all faith."[6] He added, "The Christian Church does not invite men to her fold because she contains all truth. She must not claim that, or men will soon find out its falsity ... The Church is progressive in her very essence. She is simply man sanctified by Jesus Christ."[7]

Brooks concluded his sermon by appealing to his listeners' minds and persuading them to act. Touching on the article's title, he stated, "We must make what we are to be out of what we are already. Evolution is not atheism ... We can't be nearer to God than when helping a miserable fellow-creature, for we can't conceive of God doing any more."[8] The article ended with Brooks's final sentence: "All can bring something, and though it be little it will be enough for Christ to multiply into the full fruition of a holy life."[9]

More years passed until The Times mentioned him again. In an April 13, 1882 article on John F. Slater, a wealthy Connecticut textile manufacturer whose family's business benefited from Southern slavery, and his gift of one

2. "Evolution Not Atheism."
3. "Evolution Not Atheism."
4. "Evolution Not Atheism."
5. "Evolution Not Atheism."
6. "Evolution Not Atheism."
7. "Evolution Not Atheism."
8. "Evolution Not Atheism."
9. "Evolution Not Atheism."

million dollars[10] for the creation of a corporation that would assist in the education of formerly enslaved people. The article lists several of the trustees, including former President Rutherford B. Hayes; US Supreme Court Chief Justice Morrison Remick Waite; William E. Dodge, a mining operator and philanthropist; and Phillips Brooks, who was described as "the eloquent liberal Episcopal preacher of Boston." Along with Dodge, the article described the two as "synonymous with live, energetic, and broad philanthropy, in the estimation of the whole country."[11] Brooks's prominence had expanded beyond his reputation as a preacher to include philanthropy, and his solid character buoyed the donation of atonement and reparation.

Four more years passed before The Times mentioned Brooks again. In December 1886, the Times reviewed Brooks's forthcoming book, *Twenty Sermons*. The article described him as "the chief Broad Church leader."[12] It also noted his controversial proposal at the 1885 Episcopal General Convention in Chicago to "send fraternal greetings to the Congregationalists, in session in Chicago at the same time."[13] The Times described Brooks physically: "The Rector of Trinity Church, Boston, is one of the sons of Anak" (a reference to his height of more than six feet and weight of as much as three hundred pounds).[14] The article continues, "In [Brooks's] case *orator nascitur, non fit*,[15] is true, and they who have heard him preach aver that his eloquence is like the sweeping torrent on the mountainside, which carries everything before and with it. They also are confident that his personal presence adds special force."[16] The Times now gave a clearer description of Phillips. They positioned him within the Episcopal Church's nineteenth-century parties and illustrated his willingness to push the Church ecumenically but controversially as he politically played to one of his Bostonian constituencies, namely, the Congregationalists. The Times, then, lampooned Brooks's size,

---

10. Worth approximately $31,000,000 in 2025.

11. "Educating the Freedmen." See also the University of Virginia Arts and Sciences, Exploration in Black Leadership, https://blackleadership.virginia.edu/glossary-terms/slater-fund-john-f; and Alexander, *The Slater and Jeanes Funds*.

12. "Pulpit Oratory of To-Day."

13. "Pulpit Oratory of To-Day."

14. "Pulpit Oratory of To-Day."

15. The Latin phrase translates, "An orator is born, not made."

16. "Pulpit Oratory of To-Day."

body shaming him by alluding to the "sons of Anak," who were considered descendants of the Nephilim, the mysterious Old Testament creatures.[17]

The Times article added a careful critique of Brooks's sermons and preaching ability. The article stated, "Great as he is as an orator he seeks to furnish plain, sensible teaching. His style lacks polish somewhat, but is everywhere marked by energy, fervid thought and an earnest desire to reach the hearts and conscience of his hearers."[18] The Times acknowledged the friction Brooks caused the High Church party within the Episcopal Church:

> In speaking of the Episcopal Church he says: 'There are some of her children who love to call her in exclusive phrase The American Church. She is not that . . . If our church does especial work in our country it must be by the especial and peculiarness way in which she is able to bear that witness, not by any fiction of an apostolical succession in her ministry, which gives to them alone a right to bear such witness. There is no such peculiar privilege of commission to her or any other body.'[19]

By highlighting this specific sermon, The Times highlighted Brooks's penchant to speak his mind, his positioning of himself above his denomination, and his ever-focus on preaching the Gospel to Americans. However, The Times also noted, "Dr. Brooks shows in most of his sermons loyal adherence to the teaching of the church of which he is a minister." Brooks's reputation for questioning church doctrine would get him into trouble. He would put his toe over the line but not his entire foot.

Prior to the 1891 episcopal election, The Times wrote of Brooks thrice. On July 7, 1889, The Times published an article from the *Boston Home Journal*, amounting to journalistic puffery. It started, "Perhaps no man in this city comes so near to living up to the ideal overestimated."[20] The article concluded, "There can be but one in regard to the place [Brooks] has in the affections of the world or of the wonderful good that his remarkable life has done in the world, which has too few good examples and where too few men live up to the ideal that one has of what the life of the clergy should be."[21]

The next article reported on his noonday sermon at Trinity Church, Manhattan, noting, "For the first time in the history of the parish the public

17. See Genesis 6:4 and Numbers 13:33.
18. "Pulpit Oratory of To-Day."
19. "Pulpit Oratory of To-Day."
20. "Phillips Brooks."
21. "Phillips Brooks."

were permitted to occupy the choir stalls in the chancel, while hundreds were turned away, unable to gain admission to the church." Brooks again edged toward controversy, preaching, "All men are essentially by their nature children of God."[22] A statement that downplayed humanity's sinful nature and fallen state. The article concluded with Brooks's statement: "When [a person] is willing to give up his sins, to repent, and to grieve over them, and seek after the great love and mercy and welcome of God, may he hope to come into the full measure of the Christian liberty which is in Christ Jesus."[23] In this statement, Brooks obscured his denominational teaching, which emphasized salvation as complete reconciliation with God, not a progressive movement toward freedom.

The final article was published about a year later. Drawing from a *Boston Journal* article, The Times highlighted Brooks's tachylalia. The article began, "Two hundred and forty words a minute, four words every second, is a rate of speed which seems almost beyond the power articulation."[24] The article dryly concluded, "The business men, for whom the service was especially designed, had been assured that the discourse would be short, and so it was in time, for it was finished in twenty-five minutes"[25] during which Brooks's spoke some 6,000 words. Phillips's notoriety, and The New York Times coverage waffled from the sober to the amusing. The newspaper happily highlighted Brooks's controversial opinions and unusual characteristics and showed him to be a capable and caring pastor and person.

THE 1891 EPISCOPAL ELECTION

By 1891, Phillips Brooks was known throughout the Episcopal Church and idolized in Boston. As Rachel Wenner Gardner noted earlier, his eulogy of President Lincoln brought him national notoriety. He preached to schoolboys and Queen Victoria of England.[26] He gave lectures on preaching that, as Ruthanna Hooke noted in her chapter, still have relevance. Brooks preached before thousands on any Sunday and to standing-room-only crowds in New York City churches. His fame did not prevent him from individual pastoral care, teaching the gospels to and pastoring the young

22. "Phillips Brooks."
23. "Phillips Brooks."
24. "Boston's Fast-Speaking Preacher."
25. "Boston's Fast-Speaking Preacher."
26. Allen, *Phillips Brooks*, 346.

blind and deaf girl, Helen Keller.[27] No one denied Brooks's positive qualities, but he had risen almost above his denomination, which brought great scrutiny.

On March 9, 1891, Benjamin Henry Paddock, the bishop of Massachusetts, died, and soon after, the push for his successor began. Brooks's first pastor and primary mentor, the Reverend Dr. Alexander H. Vinton, then Rector of All Saints Church, Worchester, Massachusetts, nominated Brooks to be Paddock's successor and sixth bishop of Massachusetts.[28] While Brooks's popularity in Boston and the Diocese of Massachusetts was strong, some corners of the Episcopal Church thought his potential election represented serious concerns to the denomination and the American church as a whole.

By April 6th, The Times reported on the final list of three candidates, Brooks and two others, and the opposition to Brooks. The Times reported, "While may would like to elect Dr. Brooks as a compliment for his earnest labors, there is a strong undercurrent of feeling against his religious ideas, which have become so broad that it is a question with some whether the choice of him as a spiritual leader would be a wise step." As noted previously, Brooks was a liberal Broad Church party leader with strong ecumenical tendencies. His views of apostolic succession, among other issues, presented problems for some bishops who identified strongly with the succession's tie to the first Christian leaders.

The Times article illustrated Brooks's errant ways. It stated, "His liberal views took expression last Good Friday, when he occupied the pulpit of the new Old South Church (Congregational) with a number of clergymen of different denominations, and his course on this occasion excited much comment."[29] The group of clergymen were from neighboring Copley Square churches, including from the Congregational, Unitarian, and Baptist churches.[30] The fraternization of denominations was frowned upon at the time, and the inclusion of Unitarian ministers at the event pushed some Episcopalians to think that Phillips was a heretic. The concluding comments on Brooks alluded to a growing problem for the great Boston preacher: "It is hinted that should he be elected the House of Bishops, which much confirm any candidate, would be likely to ask some searching questions before

---

27. See https://helenkellerintl.org/who-we-are/helen-keller.
28. Lambert, "The Effects of Broad Churchmanship on Public Worship," 84.
29. "To Succeed Bishop Paddock."
30. Allen, *Life and Letters*, 3:405.

granting confirmation."³¹ Trouble was brewing for Brooks that would not fade just because the diocesan convention elected him bishop.

Two days before the Massachusetts diocesan convention and bishop election, The Times published an article discussing a lecture in Boston regarding biblical criticism and the coming Episcopal bishop election. At the talk, the biblical criticism proponent "had clearly set forth the human element in the Bible."³² The article next turned to the election, focusing primarily on efforts to elect Brooks and its consequences. First, it noted, "Adherents of other Churches have an interest in the question that they would not have were any other man's election in question. For selfish reasons many of them hope that he may fail of election, for they concede that his election will wonderfully strengthen the Episcopal Church in Massachusetts."³³ The article discussed the Broad and Low Churchmen's efforts to gather votes for Brooks and then discussed the strong opposition from the Massachusetts Church Union (High Church). The article stated, "They cannot forgive him his breadth and Christian charity, his disregard of the forms and minor doctrines of his Church; they fear that he is disloyal to what they believe to be Christianity, and so they will probably go into the convention and as obstructionists, prevent his election."³⁴ The church party lines were deeply dug, and the article suspected a pitched battle for the bishopric would ensue at the convention.

On May 1st, The Times reported the results in two articles, one gave biographical details, and the other outlined his controversial positions. Of the 184 voting clergy, Brooks received 92 votes to Satterlee's 58. Of the 109 lay delegates, Brooks received 55 votes to Satterlee's 32.³⁵ Brooks received enough votes in the first round of voting to be elected the sixth bishop of the Episcopal Diocese of Massachusetts. One article stated his liberal views: "Dr. Brooks is noted for his liberal or Low Church views, and he has frequently preached in churches of other denominations than his own. It is his broad sympathy with every Christian effort that has made him popular beyond denominational limits."³⁶ The second article announced that the election was a "surprise" to people within and outside of the Episcopal Church. The article explained the outcome was on the one hand due to

31. "To Succeed Bishop Paddock."
32. "Roused to Thought."
33. "Roused to Thought."
34. "Roused to Thought."
35. "Bishop Paddock's Successor."
36. "Bishop Paddock's Successor."

"hero worship" but also because Brooks was known as a "Broad Churchman," and as such "he was supported in this capacity by clergymen and laymen who thought the Episcopal Church was in need of broadening."

The second article analyzed the impact of Brooks's election. It stated, "The nuts of Massachusetts churchmanship in the past has not been so much Broad as Low,"[37] and then reminded its readers of Brooks's core problem: "Dr. Brooks, in the matter of fraternizing with ministers of other denominations, at least, has gone much beyond the practice of his brother clergymen, and much beyond what most of his supporters were prepared to sanction."[38] As the article noted, his supporters had addressed the issue: "In fact, it was argued in his favor that as a Bishop he was likely to be more 'conservative' than he had been as the rector of Trinity."[39] However, the article concluded, "Dr. Brooks is beloved for his hearty and manly and outspoken conduct, and outspokenness is not an especially Episcopal qualification."[40] The article feared that Brooks would continue his ways, which do not embody appropriate episcopal temperament.

The Times also gave space for Brooks's supporters. On May 4th, The Times reported on a sermon by a supporter of biblical criticism and Christian unity, the Reverend R. Heber Newton, rector of All Souls' Church, Manhattan. The article explained, "Mr. Newton prefaced his sermon by a reference to the election of the Rev. Phillips Brooks of Boston to a Bishopric."[41] Newton argued, "The choice of such a broad-minded, charitable thinker was a great consolation to others of the same school who were suffering discouragement here."[42] He claimed Brooks was a man of charity, which is "the foundation of religion itself, the life in which all religions are made one."[43]

By May 9th, The Times reported that Brooks accepted the diocesan election results. In a brief letter to the diocesan standing committees and bishops, he graciously acknowledged receiving the official notice and thanked all involved. Brooks also recognized the approaching Episcopal Church approval process, writing, "Should the election by the convention

37. "Bishop Phillips Brooks."
38. "Bishop Phillips Brooks."
39. "Bishop Phillips Brooks."
40. "Bishop Phillips Brooks."
41. "A Plea for Charity."
42. "A Plea for Charity."
43. "A Plea for Charity."

receive the indorsement which our Church demands, I shall accept the responsible and sacred office."[44]

THE ELECTION CONTROVERSY

Eleven days later, The Times reported on the first diocese to decline Brooks's election. The Standing Committee of the [Newark] Diocese reported, "It had unanimously refused to consent to the consecration of the Rev. Dr. Phillips Brooks as Bishop of Massachusetts. His views on some questions of Church policy and discipline are regarded with disfavor by the committee."[45] In his annual diocesan address, Bishop Starkey also addressed their refusal, stating,

> I admit that there is a wide range in the matter of religious thought. But there are those in the Church who have denied and taught others to deny, much within those limits. Christ truly arose from the dead, says the Article (A reference to the fourth of the Thirty-Nine Articles of Religion), and again took His body, flesh, and bones, and ascended into heaven. No doubt there is a mystery in this, but it is beyond all question a trifling with language when men who have no knowledge on the subject themselves are led by their teachers within the Church to deny this Article.[46]

Although he did not name Brooks directly, his criticism was obviously directed at Brooks.

A quick backlash ensued. The next day, The Times reported on the convention's next day, stating in the subtitle, "His Friends in the Newark Diocese Enter a Protest."[47] A group of Brooks's supporters had prepared a written response overnight and handed it out at the convention's door. The statement read,

> Though we ourselves are not wholly in sympathy with Mr. Brooks, we feel that many in this convention must regret the consent to the confirmation of the foremost preacher in the Church, a man of absolute integrity of character, of supreme gifts, of mobile nature, a man selected by a large majority of all churchman in his own State, a man who latterly was chosen as Lenten preacher in New York, a

44. "The Rev. Dr. Brooks Accepts."
45. "Against Phillips Brooks."
46. "Against Phillips Brooks."
47. "Phillips Brooks's Case."

man of commanding influence in the intellectual part of this land, a man against whose theology or the essentials of churchmanship nothing can be said, should be refused by the Standing Committee of the Diocese of Newark.[48]

In many respects, Newark's refusal and the counterargument formed the basis of the Massachusetts episcopate battle.

The diocesan count for and against Brooks rolled in over the next few weeks. On May 21st, The Times noted that Iowa's standing committee objected to Brooks. The next day, New York's Standing Committee announced its assent to Brooks.[49] The committee stated, "There never has been, nor could be, a question in respect to the orthodoxy of Phillips Brooks or his loyalty to the Episcopal Church." They concluded, "There is no objection, in its estimation, to the confirmation of the eminent divine, pulpit orator, and theologian named by the Diocese of Massachusetts for the elevation to the episcopate, it is tantamount to serving a notice to the other dioceses in the Church that no substantial foundation exists for the opposition to Dr. Brooks."[50]

More Standing Committees reported, and support for Brooks continued. The Times reported on May 23rd that Albany, Rhode Island, Indiana, Missouri, and North Carolina approved Brooks. On May 24th, a Letter to the Editor from Rev. John P. Appleton, Rector of Grace Church, Nutley, New Jersey, appeared in The Times, titled "Narrow, Suspicious Orthodoxy: It is Time for the Episcopal Church to Broaden Out."[51] Appleton addressed the three main objections to Brooks. He started with one previously mentioned in this chapter: "Dr. Brooks does not believe in the necessity of the third order (the episcopate) of the ministry to the existence of the church." Appleton defends Brooks's view by noting, "This view has been held by many distinguished Bishops." He adds that the Anglican Communion has spoken, stating, "The declaration has no serious meaning at all, involves no theory of the episcopate but the simple acceptance of it as a fact and so it has been generally interpreted."

The other two objections included a Christian tenant and an ecumenical viewpoint. Appleton stated that the second objection to Brooks is "whether he believes in the divinity of Christ in the incarnation."[52] Appleton's

48. "Phillips Brooks's Case."
49. "Favors Phillips Brooks."
50. "Favors Phillips Brooks."
51. Appleton, "Narrow, Suspicious, Orthodoxy."
52. Appleton, "Narrow, Suspicious Orthodoxy."

response was simple: "It is inconceivable that one who is familiar with Dr. Brooks's sermons should fail to see that his loyalty to Christ as Son of God, his adoration of Him, his obedient following of Him, make the very spirit of his life."[53] The final objection was his alleged affiliation, association, and fealty with Unitarians. Appleton noted, "It is said he has shown his sympathy with Unitarians by participating with them in union services." Appleton countered, "The objection appears most unreasonable. I suppose we may all have sympathy with what is positive in Unitarianism or with Judaism, for the matter of that. To call that 'fellowship with unbelievers" seems a strange misuse of the terms."[54] Despite the passionate and reasoned support for Brooks, the Episcopal Diocese of Chicago did not indorse Brooks.[55]

By the end of May, the process began to turn ugly. The Times reported daily on Brooks's indorsement progress. Connecticut unanimously consented to Brooks, but Quincy unanimously declined.[56] The coordinated campaign against Brooks by the Boston High Church party began to unravel. The Times reported on May 29th, "It is just learned here that members of the Standing Committees of several Episcopal diocese in this county . . . have been in receipt of various anonymous circulars and pamphlets mailed from Boston."[57] The documents contained information, which "is said to be, in may respects, false and misleading."[58] The Times reported on Brooks's sermon on May 30: "Nobody who heard Dr. Brooks last Sunday morning as he preached on the Trinity in Trinity Church on *Trinity* Sunday could ever dare charge him with Unitarianism. He seemingly went out of his way to put himself on the record as a Trinitarian."[59] By June 2nd, The Times stated that the Diocese of Virginia had given unanimous consent.[60]

By the end of the week, the Times gave an update on the tally. Twenty-six dioceses supported Brooks: "New York, Albany, Rhode Island, Tennessee, Western Missouri, Missouri, North Carolina, Ohio and Southern Ohio, Indiana, Pennsylvania and Central Pennsylvania, New Jersey, Michigan, Connecticut, Maryland, Nebraska, Minnesota, Long Island, California,

---

53. Appleton, "Narrow, Suspicious Orthodoxy."
54. Appleton, "Narrow, Suspicious Orthodoxy."
55. "Did not Indorse Phillips Brooks."
56. "They Vote for Phillips Brooks," May 27, 1891; and "Opposed to Phillips Brooks."
57. "The Case of Phillips Brooks."
58. "The Case of Phillips Brooks."
59. "Liberal Leaven Working."
60. "They Vote for Phillips Brooks," June 2, 1891.

Virginia and West Virginia, Kentucky, Kansas, Delaware, and Louisiana." Those dioceses against him included "Newark, Iowa, Milwaukee, Mississippi, Chicago, Texas, Maine, Springfield, and Fond du Lac." Brooks needed one more Standing Committee's support. Who would it be?

DE COSTA AND CHEVALLIER

While waiting for another Standing Committee's decision, the curious case of the Rev. Dr. De Costa's campaign against Brooks took center stage. On June 3rd, The Times reported on De Costa's vehement opposition to Brooks.[61] Since 1881, De Costa had been the rector of the Church of St. John the Evangelist in New York City but was a native of the Boston area. He had alleged that an unnamed correspondent, personal friend, and admirer of Brooks from Boston had written him regarding Brooks. The communication stated that Dr. Brooks believes that "the miraculous birth of our Lord is nowise essential."[62] By June 7th, The Times reported that a Miss A.A. Chevallier hastily joined De Costa in his crusade against Brooks, which is "dictated purely by personal feelings."[63]

Chevallier was a mysterious figure. The Times reported on a *San Francisco Chronicle* article toward the end of June. A reporter found Miss Alzire A. Chevallier in "charming seclusion in one of the most novel and picturesque mountain retreats in California,"[64] near Santa Rosa, owned by Thomas Lake Harris, a Universalist minister, spiritualist, and commune founder. Chevallier told the reporter, "I do not myself think that Phillips Brooks can properly assume the Bishopric. He is broader than the canons and dogma he is bound there to uphold. He would, too, occupy a much narrower field of useful work and influence than he does now."[65] She stated, "He is my friend and was my pastor for many years . . . Dr. Brooks is a noble, great-hearted man, and he is always honest and sincere."[66] With the anonymous correspondent fully outed, the Standing Committees and bishops ignored Dr. De Costa's further criticism.

61. "Good Words for Dr. Brooks.
62. "Dr. De Costa's Correspondent."
63. "Dr. De Costa's Correspondent."
64. "Dr. De Costa's Adviser."
65. "Dr. De Costa's Adviser."
66. "Dr. De Costa's Adviser."

BISHOP BROOKS

During June and July, Brooks's future was sorted. The Standing Committee approvals for Brooks continued to grow. On June 11th, South Carolina unanimously supported Brooks.[67] Followed by East Carolina the next day.[68] The final tally was reported on June 28th. Thirty-seven dioceses voted in favor of Brooks, and fifteen voted against him.[69] However, Brooks's battle for the episcopate had not concluded. The bishops themselves had to vote for or against Brooks. Several weeks passed. On July 10th, The Times announced, "Surprise has been felt by some people, particularly by the loyal adherents of Rev. Dr. Phillips Brooks, that there has been so much delay on the part of the Bishops in recording their votes in the matter of the confirmation of his election as Bishop."[70]

On July 12th, a Letter to the Editor sought to dissuade any remaining opposition to Brooks. The letter stated, "The opposition to his confirmation came from sticklers for the enforcement of the rules of the Church, for some of which Dr. Brooks as a Presbyter has shown little regard."[71] The author suggested that opposition to Brooks was, in fact, "admonishing the new Bishop to be more careful than the rector of Trinity had been."[72] The author assured them: "There need be no fear that Dr. Brooks will repeat as a Bishop his caprices of independence as a clergyman . . . that as a man he will do honor to the episcopate."[73] That sentiment seemed to echo the feelings of the bishops, and on July 24th, The Times announced Phillips Brooks's consecration date as October 14th.[74]

Brooks never addressed the accusations. He chose silence over a tit-for-tat that would have ensued if he had confronted his detractors in public or in the press. At the post-consecration dinner, The Times reported on Brooks's "half hour impassioned address."[75] He stated, "No matter what a Church believes, if it does the thing the soul of the world feels must be done,

---

67. "They Vote for Phillips Brooks," June 11, 1891.
68. "For Phillips Brooks."
69. "Voting for Phillips Brooks."
70. "Phillips Brooks Has not Been Confirmed by the Bishops."
71. "Letter to the Editor No. 6."
72. "Letter to the Editor No. 6."
73. "Letter to the Editor No. 6."
74. "To be Bishop Brooks in October."
75. "A Typical Boston Week."

if it brings its hope to its hopelessness, if it puts its strength upon is weakness, its love upon its misery, its joy upon its sorrow, the soul of the world will recognize its help and come to it and build it up."[76] Brooks's silence did not mean he agreed with his critics or felt the burn of admonishment enough to change his ways. He refrained from addressing the criticism for tactical reasons.

Less than a year later, the attacks on Brooks resumed. On September 15, 1892, The Times reported, "The Right Rev. Dr. Seymour, Bishop of the Diocese of Springfield, has addressed an open letter to the Right Rev. Dr. William C. Doane, Bishop of Albany." The Times explained, "The letter is a continuation of the attacks upon the distinguished Boston preacher which began when he was a candidate for the episcopate." Bishop Seymour's letter was lengthy, explaining how and why Brooks was a heretic. Seymour accused Brooks of Pelagianism, Arianism, and Congregationalism. He had withheld his criticism for as long as he could, hoping that his supporters were right that Bishop Brooks would respect the Episcopal Church's canons and teachings.[77] In Bishop Seymour's opinion, Brooks had not. As stated in the conclusion of his letter, Seymour's accusations were the same as those mentioned earlier in this chapter.[78] Doane ignored Seymour.

CONCLUSION

No question Brooks was a liberal. His views on biblical criticism, ecumenism, and the individual's agency to interpret biblical scripture stood against the views of many in the Episcopal High Church party. He also had ecumenical tendencies far beyond his colleague's views. Many Episcopal Church clergy maintained a keen eye on the church's rituals and viewed other denominational practices with suspicion. Thus, Brooks's open heart toward all Christians and people of faith, regardless of denomination or faith tradition, made them uncomfortable. Brooks's and the other Broad Churchmen's liberal views toward the new biblical criticism movement appalled his more traditional and conservative Episcopal colleagues.

However, Brooks was always Christocentric. As Ruthanna Hooke stated, he sought Christ and always preached Christ. He believed in and taught others that Christ was active and present in the world. That is exactly what

76. "A Typical Boston Week."
77. Seymour, *An Open Letter*, 1–2.
78. Seymour, *An Open Letter*, 144–46.

his mother had taught him, and Brooks never wavered from her teaching. The person who wrote "O Little Town of Bethlehem" must have been Christocentric. Karen Swallow Prior noted in her chapter: "Brooks conveys this theological insight marvelously and simply in the hymn with the plea addressed to Christ to "enter in" and "be born in us." Paul's expression from Colossians 2:6–12 of being *alive in Christ* represents Brooks's famous hymn's theology and fully represents his view of Christianity, which is an orthodox, traditional Christian view.

Today's readers may struggle with Brooks's controversies. They seem banal and pedestrian. Seminarians today learn biblical criticism and exegetical techniques fundamental to modern interpretation of scripture. They study world religions while sitting with members of different Christian denominations. Many small-town and big-city churches share the Good Friday liturgy and pulpit with various pastors and priests. Hospital and military chaplains work side-by-side with leaders from a variety of faith traditions to serve the needs of the sick and injured. Phillips Brooks was beloved because, in addition to his eloquence, he thought broadly and remained open to seeing where Christ was working in the world.

His faults invariably tripped him up. The Boston Latin and Harvard-educated Boston Brahmin had classist tendencies. He was from the elite class of New England, and his elitist attitudes showed up at Virginia Seminary. His opinions of his professors and classmates, found in his letters, expressed his snobbery. He frequently spoke about the *common man*. Brooks was not common and not raised to be common. So, he could not help but see the world through his privileged eyes.

He held strong opinions about the Episcopal Church and Christianity and fought against the Episcopal Church's biases and prejudices. When asked about controversial issues, he did not use political tact. He spoke plainly about biblical criticism, aware that his High Church party colleagues disagreed. He minced no words about his questions about the necessity and centrality of apostolic succession and the episcopate. Since he preached often without a prepared text or limited notes, he did not take the space and time to reflect on what he would say. Thus, at times, his words, no matter how quickly spoken, made news and offended some.

All in all, Brooks's controversial statements were not particularly wayward. His questioning of the episcopate highlighted the importance of one's individual relationship to Jesus, not mediated through strict rituals and doctrine. He opened the doors of the Episcopal Church to welcome many more people than the staid elite. Brooks was also able to reach beyond Christianity to the Jewish tradition. After his death in January 1893, a remembrance service was held in New York City on February 13th. Rabbi Gustav Gottheil of Temple Emanu-El, a reformed congregation, remembered Brooks, saying, "My brethren, finding a man in his lofty station as a ruler of his Church, illumined by the light of a pure and true and strong humanity, could not but revere him, and now that he is in his grave, cannot but thank God that such a Christian bishop has lived in our land."[79] Phillips Brooks abided with many, many people serving them as Christ loved him.

BIBLIOGRAPHY

"Against Phillips Brooks." *New York Times*, May 20, 1891.
Alexander, Will W. *The Slater and Jeanes Funds: An Educator's Approach to a Difficult Social Problem*, Washington, DC: The Trustees of the John F. Slater Fund, 1934, https://ia800908.us.archive.org/21/items/slaterjeanesfund00alex/slaterjeanesfund00alex.pdf.
Allen, Alexander, V. G. *The Life and Letters of Phillips Brooks*. Vol. 3. New York: Dutton, 1901.
———. *Phillips Brooks (1835–1893): Memoires of His Life with Extracts from his Letters and Note-Books*. New York: Dutton, 1907.
Appleton, John P. "Narrow, Suspicious, Orthodoxy: It is Time for the Episcopal Church to Broaden Out." Letters to the Editor, *New York Times*, May 24, 1891.
"Bishop Paddock's Successor." *New York Times*, May 1, 1891.
"Bishop Phillips Brooks." *New York Times*, May 1, 1891.
"Boston's Fast-Speaking Preacher." *New York Times*, February 22, 1891.
"The Case of Phillips Brooks." *New York Times*, May 29, 1891.
"Did not Indorse Phillips Brooks." *New York Times*, May 26, 1891.
"Dr. De Costa's Correspondent." *New York Times*, June 7, 1891.
"Educating The Freedmen: The Charitable Purpose of John F. Slater." *New York Times*, April 13, 1882.
"Evolution Not Atheism." *New York Times*, April 29, 1879.
"Favors Phillips Brooks." *New York Times*, May 22, 1891.
"For Phillips Brooks." *New York Times*, June 12, 1891.
"Good Words for Dr. Brooks: Dr. De Costa's Opposition Meets with No Sympathy Here." *New York Times*, June 3, 1891.
Gottheil, Gustav. "Address." In *Service in Memory of Phillips Brooks*, 12–15. New York: Thomas Whittaker, 2 and 3 Bible House, 1893.
Lambert, Paul E. "The Effects of Broad Churchmanship on Public Worship: William R. Huntington, Alexander H. Vinton and Ritual in Low-Church Worcester, Massachusetts, 1863–1902." *Anglican and Episcopal History* 67 (1998) 69–92.
"Letter to the Editor No. 6." *New York Times*, July 12, 1891.
"Liberal Leaven Working: Boston Interested in the Theological Battles." *New York Times*, May 31, 1891.

---

79. Gustave Gottheil, "Address," 14.

"Opposed to Phillips Brooks." *New York Times*, May 31, 1891.
"Phillips Brooks: A Couple of Anecdotes of the Great Boston Preacher." *New York Times*, July 7, 1889.
"Phillips Brooks's Case." *New York Times*, May 21, 1891.
"Phillips Brooks Has not Been Confirmed by the Bishops." *New York Times*, July 10, 1891.
"A Plea for Charity." *New York Times*, May 4, 1891.
"Pulpit Oratory of To-Day." *New York Times*, December 19, 1886.
"The Rev. Dr. Brooks Accepts." *New York Times*, May 9, 1891.
"Roused to Thought: Boston Clergymen Interested in 'Heretics' and a Bishopric." *New York Times*, April 27, 1891.
Seymour, George Franklin. *An Open Letter to the Rt. Rev. William C. Doane*: In Reference to the Consecration of the Rt. Rev. Dr. Brooks, by the Bishop of Springfield. Springfield, IL: Rokker, 1892. https://ia800906.us.archive.org/12/items/openlettertortreooseym/openlettertortreooseym.pdf.
"They Vote for Phillips Brooks." *New York Times*, May 27, 1891.
"They Vote for Phillips Brooks." *New York Times*, June 2, 1891.
"They Vote for Phillips Brooks." *New York Times*, June 11, 1891.
"To Be Bishop Brooks in October." *New York Times*, July 24, 1891.
"To Succeed Bishop Paddock." *New York Times*, April 6, 1891.
"A Typical Boston Week." *New York Times*, November 1, 1891.
"Voting for Phillips Brooks." *New York Times*, June 28, 1891.

8

The Everlasting Light
Phillips Brooks's Legacy at the Phillips Brooks House Association

Mary Catherine Curley

AT THE NORTHWEST CORNER of Harvard Yard stands a brick building shadowed by oak trees, with three words emblazoned on its face: *Piety, Charity, and Hospitality.* The house was erected at the turn of the 20th century following Phillips Brooks's death, a memorial effort funded and organized by his colleagues and friends.

Since 1904, the building has housed the Phillips Brooks House Association, a collective of student organizations devoted to public service. Student-run programs serving neighborhoods in Boston and Cambridge have provided adult, advocacy, after school, housing, medical, mentoring and summer services to thousands of people ever since. The building has been home to other social justice efforts over the years, including the university's first women's center and, mostly recently, programs housed through the Harvard Center for Public Service and Engaged Scholarship. By 1973, PBHA incorporated as a 501(c)(3) nonprofit. Today, it is home to dozens of programs, including the Summer Urban Program, a neighborhood-based network of summer camps that enrolls eight hundred children from low-income families and provides summer employment to over a hundred local teens; the Harvard Square Homeless Shelter and Y2Y, two shelters which provide beds and hot meals to adults and young people experiencing homelessness, and English language classes for almost six hundred adults. Not only is PBHA the largest student-run nonprofit in the country, it has run community-based programs in some Boston neighborhoods for decades—so long that a single family might have sent two generations to the same PBHA summer camp, or a former child participants in programming grow up to run the program they once attended.

Every day, students entering the house pass a bronze bust of Phillips Brooks, and a plaque that reads *This House is dedicated to Piety Charity and Hospitality—in grateful memory of Phillips Brooks*. Many are on their way to a community meeting, picking up a megaphone to take over to a protest, or making photocopies for the after-school program they're running in Boston. Some are engaged in work that may define their lives, discovering a calling to work in education, housing, or organizing. Still others are facing questions of what kind of person they want to be and what kind of life they want to live, challenging each other's notions of justice, equality, and solidarity. Years after graduation, PBHA alumni consistently name their in-depth service experiences as transformative. In the words of one 2003 alumnus, "I was really active in PBHA during a time in my life where I was figuring out the person I was going to be. The experiences and opportunities for reflection I had with PBHA made service part of my identity—for the rest of my life, I've asked myself whether what I'm doing makes the world better, and how. This is how I think of who I am."

When the building was first built in Brooks's name, he had passed away only seven years prior, and his friends and students felt strongly about what his legacy on the campus should be. Before his death, Brooks had joined other university preachers in requesting a new building on Harvard's campus specifically to house religious groups, to be "generously used for all the various public interests of university life, and should unite and strengthen many undertakings which now rather tend to divide the forces which make for good among the students."[1] His close friend Edwin Hale Abbott, who fundraised for the building following his death, emphasized Brooks's wish "to stimulate spiritual life other than the intellectual work of these young fellows," and urged classmates to help establish a building that might serve as "the very heart of the college, and the home of its religious and spiritual life in all those forms."[2] Later, at the building's opening, Rob-

1. Gotlieb, "The Friendship and the House," 37–48.
2. Gotlieb, "Friendship and the House," 37–48.

ert Treat Paine declared an even more ambitious vision for the house: that it might represent "the great elective of spiritual communion; to recognize as the fundamental fact of human existence that man is made in the image of God."[3]

Over a century later, Phillips Brooks House both embodies and resists this vision, in fascinating and unexpected ways. The organization housed within the building has long declared itself officially secular, and students volunteering there might easily come and go without ever learning who the building was named for. As a former student and staff member at PBHA, this author was at first unsure what connections might be found between Phillips Brooks's own reflections on service, the original vision for the house, and its current work. However, in his sermons to Harvard students—specifically, his final address in Appleton Chapel and his reflections on "the beauty of a life of service"—one can hear messages that resonate powerfully today with PBHA's unique model of service learning and community action.

DEDICATING THE HOUSE

On January 23, 1900, on the seventh anniversary of Phillips Brooks's passing, his friends and colleagues gathered in Harvard Yard to dedicate the newly erected Phillips Brooks House.[4] The group had been hard at work on the project for the past seven years, fundraising, planning, and even convincing the city of Cambridge to adjust the streets to improve the new building's positioning.[5]

Brooks's connections with Harvard extended decades. He attended the university as an undergraduate, earning his degree in 1855. Charles Eliot, who would go on to serve as Harvard president, described him as "recognized by teachers and comrades alike as an affectionate and high-minded youth of large promise, particularly as a writer." However, it was not until Brooks discovered his calling as a preacher and returned to Harvard in this capacity that this "large promise" found its outlet.

As a young man, Brooks had not always been confident, or even clear about his calling. He later described Harvard as a place "where men studied

---

3. Paine, *Phillips Brooks House*.
4. Paine, *Phillips Brooks House*.
5. Paine, *Phillips Brooks House*.

hard, but said nothing about faith."[6] His attempts at a teaching career in Boston failed, before he decided in the summer of 1856 to become an ordained minister.[7] He was thirty years old when he delivered a sermon in Philadelphia two days after the assassination of Abraham Lincoln, on Easter Sunday—marking a decisive turning point in his career. Three months later, he would be invited to provide the invocation at Harvard's commemoration ceremony for students and alumni killed in the war. By then, Charles Eliot's description of Brooks was decidedly different; he was a "young prophet risen up in Israel."[8]

Later on, Brooks would serve as a University Chaplain at Harvard, as well as an Overseer, and become a beloved figure among the undergraduates who came to hear him preach. He declined the university's offer to make him a professor, choosing instead to focus on his work as a parish priest in Boston.[9] In his remarks at the Brooks House dedication, Robert Treat Paine, founder of the Associated Charities of Boston and chairman of the planning committee for the house, recalled how Brooks "delighted to offer to undergraduates counsels of inspiration in wondrous sympathy with the lives and hopes and joys of robust youth."[10] Through sermons and conversations, Brooks emphasized to students a spiritual calling that might otherwise have been lost amid the demands and rewards of a Harvard education—a risk that Paine hoped the newly erected Phillips Brooks House might help to address.

"To this interesting variety of buildings," Paine declared, "suggesting so many studies and careers, the life of Phillips Brooks has prompted his friends to add this Phillips Brooks House, in hopes to strengthen the religious spirit of Harvard, always so staunch from its first Puritan origin, to increase the study of holy things and to make the worship of God the career of some and an essential part of the life of all." The campus already included chapels and departments in which students might study theology and religion. Paine's remarks made clear that the new house was intended not just as a generally religious space, but an expansion of "religious spirit" into other parts of life, "to make the worship of God the career of some and an essential part of the life of all." The group, after all, did not dedicate a

6. Harp, "The Young Phillips Brooks," 652–67.
7. Harp, "The Young Phillips Brooks," 652–67.
8. Clark, "Sermon by Phillips Brooks," 37–49.
9. Fallows, "The Jubilee of Phillips Brooks."
10. Paine, *Phillips Brooks House.*

seminary, or a new concentration of study, but rather, a place where a wide range of students might expand the spiritual lens through which they might view their entire lives.

In particular, Paine may have been concerned about students whose in-depth study of literature, history, or science might preclude an equally profound examination of "the wisdom of God." Here he seems to be making a distinction between a study of theology or religion, and the cultivation of a personal spiritual life. He continued, "The furious absorption of modern life, nowhere keener than in America, into never-ending business with its brilliant rewards leads men astray after false idols, closing their vision of the true God, till many of them forget, ignore or doubt, and at least, losing their spiritual powers, become spiritual wrecks . . . The elective system has grave dangers."[11] In other words, Harvard students were faced with incredible power and possibilities—but at what cost? "How can we measure adequately," Paine concluded, "the tremendous responsibility growing out of the splendid privileges of the sons of Harvard in these years?"[12]

At first glance, comparing Paine's remarks and the state of Phillips Brooks House Association today, one might assume little of the original vision remains. Certainly the house's relationship to religion is altered. But the question of spiritual life at Harvard—and the responsibility of students—remains urgent as ever in Brooks House. Even further, the tradition of service at Phillips Brooks House embraces an expansive view of spiritual life that can be understood through the writings of none other than Phillips Brooks himself.

PHILLIPS BROOKS HOUSE BEGINS

At its founding in 1904, Phillips Brooks House Association was indeed a religious institution, established through the collaboration of such groups as the Harvard Christian Association, Religious Union, and St. Paul's Catholic Club. The Student Volunteer Committee at the time, which coordinated the religious groups' volunteer efforts, had a significant membership overlap with the Harvard Young Men's Christian Association.[13] While some programs were overtly religious in nature, such as the Missions Committee, which raised funds for missionary travel and expenses abroad, much of the

11 Paine, *Phillips Brooks House*.
12. Paine, *Phillips Brooks House*.
13. Gips, "Babbling Brooks," 14.

work taken on by students at the house seemed steered by a belief expressed in the Harvard Alumni Bulletin: "that the truest religion is that which finds its expression in service."[14]

As early as 1910, PBHA leaders sought to emphasize that their work was not religious. By 1915, PBHA president W.H. Trumbull reflected, "It was not long ago that any man who was connected with the Brooks House work was considered more or less of a 'hypocrite,' if he did not happen to be religious... but how different the situation is today... In short, there is no religious compulsion. The religion is there and you can take just as little or as much as you want."[15] Later efforts in the 1920s to bring back the "religious zeal" of Brooks House did not take off with the student body, with one leader telling a friend he faced "bitter discouragement" from students every time he tried "to develop the spiritual aspects of the work."[16] By 1926, the Harvard Christian Association had dissolved, and by 1929, PBHA officially considered itself a secular organization, abolishing the Missions Committee.[17]

This resistance to a religious bent had many sources. Some students were concerned that requiring a religious motivation, even indirectly, would scare off volunteers who might otherwise be interested in the house's efforts. Others had a more philosophical concern about the "missionary spirit" that could be found in even non-religious programs, with one student criticizing the danger of seeing "charity" as "that form of service which consists in the extension of aid by the consciously fortunate to the declaredly unfortunate—'the weaker brother.' In its more extreme form this charity becomes patronizing; in its mildest form it fosters a sense of moral inequality."[18]

PBHA's history has run parallel to Harvard's and the nation's, often reflecting wider developments in political and social movements, and these trends are reflected in students' thinking around service and faith. In the 1950s and 1960s, PBHA programs inspired programs like President Kennedy's VISTA and the Peace Corps. In the 1970s, PBHA's Undergraduate Teachers Program preceded Teach for America-like models to support understaffed schools by decades; in the same period, a tenth of the men and women incarcerated in Massachusetts were receiving tutoring from PBHA's

14. Gips, "Babbling Brooks," 17.
15. Gips, "Babbling Brooks," 35.
16. Gips, "Babbling Brooks," 37.
17. Gips, "Babbling Brooks," 38.
18. Gips, "Babbling Brooks," 26.

Prisoner Education Committee. Over the decades, students and staff have debated the role that privileged Harvard students could or should play in service work or wider movements for justice. In different forms, in different years, critiques of *missionary, noblesse oblige,* or *white savior* attitudes have figured prominently in how young people have sought to understand their relationship to service, and to the communities outside Harvard's gates.

And yet, much of what Paine discussed that January day in 1900 speaks to a broader spiritual project that does sound familiar, even to a modern PBHA alum—and comes even further into focus when considering how Brooks himself spoke about service.

THE POWER OF SERVICE

For one, Paine's concern with Harvard students whose "furious absorption" with "never-ending business" has "[led them] astray after false idols" rings true to any student who has observed an increasing percentage of their classmates be recruited into investment banking, consulting, and hedge fund management. In recent years, Harvard College has articulated that its mission is "to educate the citizens and citizen-leaders for our society"—an institutional recognition that the purpose of an education is broader than mere personal gain. However, the idea that one can "direct [one's] whole soul and all their energies in such narrow paths, often towards ignoble ends" still resonates at any privileged institution. The "elective" possibilities of an elite education extend an option to *narrow* one's focus to individualist, capitalist gains, or use the power and privilege inherent in the degree to accumulate personal wealth or prestige. Students who have found another path at Harvard—many of them at PBHA—often describe having sought out something "more" or "deeper" than potential material gain or social status. In a recent alumni survey, one former PBHA student wrote, "PBHA is the only place in my entire Harvard experience that ever held me accountable [for] something beyond my own personal, material success." Another reflected, "I could feel a sense of purpose in my work there that wasn't possible in other 'extracurricular' work at Harvard that felt meaningless to me." Across generations, alumni consistently refer to PBHA as being their way out of the "Harvard bubble," a reason to leave campus and build meaningful relationships through service and advocacy, often across racial and socioeconomic lines.

Secondly, Paine's question of "how can we measure adequately the tremendous responsibility growing out of the splendid privileges of the sons of Harvard in these years?"[19] arguably looms as large today at PBHA as it did in 1900. During the development of the organization's case for support in 2014–2015, I held a number of focus groups with alumni who had been deeply involved with PBHA during their undergraduate years. The topic of how Harvard students should wield the privilege that comes with their degree and access came up again and again. If students at such a university go on to a disproportionate number of positions of power, how are they using it? What sorts of preparation for those roles might lead them to fight for justice, rather than individual gain? What does it mean for them to use their privilege to that end—both to the community at large, and to the students themselves, in their souls? Few alumni used the language of spirituality, but many returned to the idea that there was something larger than themselves worth fighting for through service and movement work, that the *tremendous responsibility* of their privilege might be worth applying in that direction, far more than money or power.

But all of the questions above can be best understood by examining Phillips Brooks's own philosophy of service, and the transformation—spiritual and otherwise—that service can make possible. In February 1893, in what would be Brooks's final sermon, he addressed an audience of Harvard students in Appleton Chapel, in Harvard's Memorial Church. He focused his remarks on scripture from John 10:10: "I came that they might have life, and have it abundantly" and quickly establishes the primacy of these words in a remarkable opening:

> Among all the words of Jesus I do not know where we shall find larger words than these. They are primitive and fundamental. They go back to the very beginning and purpose of His presence on the earth ... Behind all special things which He wanted men to do and be, behind all the great lessons which He wanted men to learn, He wanted men first of all to live ... It is deficient vitality, not excessive vitality, which makes the mischief and trouble of the world. Below the question of whether a Being is living well or living ill there is the deeper question whether he is living at all. The great hunger everywhere is for life. All unliving things are reaching up towards it. All living things are craving an increase of it.[20]

19. Paine, *Phillips Brooks House*.
20. "Last Sermon Preached by Phillips Brooks in Appleton Chapel."

The Everlasting Light

The focus on vitality and life—on *living*, rather than "living well or living ill"—echoes an earlier sermon Brooks delivered on his own philosophy of service. In that address, he argued for listeners to understand "service" not as a term of obligation, but rather "a word of freedom."[21] He associates a spiritual life, a life of service to others and to God, as a freeing, life-giving, even joyful enterprise, in stark contrast to images of Christian discipline or sacrifice.

This framing is striking especially in the context of Harvard. Brooks describes the nature of a person who is a "Life-giver," explaining that they "may or may not" be "students, artists, athletes." Rather than defined by their accomplishments or pedigree, these are people who "inspire the great primary emotions, hope, shame, desire, in the class, the College, the world in which they move." He distinguishes "Life-givers" from "Deed-doers" and "Word-Sayers." In a university context, full of high-achieving and ambitious young people, it is easy for "Deed-doing" and "Word-Saying" to be prized above other characteristics. Here, Brooks dismisses this rubric, valuing instead a more ephemeral quality, one that might be held by anyone, of any talent or background.

Brooks addresses the role of Harvard students directly. "The world has no use for this place," he declares, "unless here all that I have been trying to say to you tonight find its perpetual illustration." He acknowledges that "the world thinks that it has a use for this place," as evidenced by the university's endowment, but questions what Harvard's true purpose for existing is: "It is all nonsense to say or think that it is in order that a few privileged young men may be prepared to earn an easy living and grow rich some day above their fellow-men . . . It is, it must be, that first here and then wherever they who have been educated here may go, there may be seen a pattern and picture of the highest life of man."

With these words, Brooks hits on a question PBHA students have wrestled with ever since: what should be done with the privilege such a degree and institution bestow upon its students? What is the purpose of being handed this power? What kind of person should I become, now that I have it? Even further, some might ask: should I accept it at all, or question the offer in the first place? For generations, PBHA has been a place where students asked these questions of themselves and their classmates, and discovered alternative causes into which to channel their education and privilege. "PBHA has always had expectations of real commitment from

---

21. Brooks. *Addresses by the Right Reverend Phillips Brooks.*

the students," said a former PBHA leader and Harvard Overseer in a recent survey, comparing it to more common "one-off" service programs in which one might show up, volunteer, but fail to build a lasting, mutual relationship with the community. Another alumnus reflected on the "really high standard of what it meant to strive for justice . . . people at PBHA were not satisfied with bare-minimum, feel-good, band-aid solutions." Rather than use service as a way to feel better about their privilege, students at PBHA frequently discover that their experiences in community work lead them to question the foundations of the systems that undergirded that privilege to begin with.

SERVING THE "FELLOW-MAN"

Brooks himself was staunchly loyal to Harvard, and he did not question the means by which its wealth had been accrued. His points about what else a Harvard education might offer were instead focused on what type of life a person might live, given what they invest time and attention into at critical junctures of their lives. In "The Beauty of a Life of Service," he compares the idea of a life lived for oneself, and a life lived for others, interpreting Jesus's words at the Last Supper, "For their sakes I sanctify myself, that they might also be sanctified" as "I am my best, not simply for myself, but for the world."[22] In this understanding, service is not just what one *should* do out of a moral imperative, nor does it indicate a simple sacrifice of self interest for others. Rather, service expands one's world, increasing possibility and connection in a way that transforms the person serving.

Brooks describes a man who "has his soul absolutely full of the desire to help his fellow-man. He peers into those faces as he goes, and sees the divine possibility that is in them, and he sees the divine nature everywhere . . ." and compares him to his hypothetical friend who "is asking how he may be a little richer in his miserable wealth when the day sinks." In Brooks's example, the man living for himself finds himself living a smaller and smaller life, spiritually and emotionally, despite the increase of his wealth. Compared to his friend who finds "divine possibility" through service, the possibilities of the self-concerned man shrink with each passing day, his imagination growing impoverished. The imagery Brooks uses here is striking: "peer[ing] into those faces" of his neighbors. One might imagine, by contrast, the rich man turning his eyes away from others, or

22. Brooks, *Addresses by the Right Reverend Phillips Brooks*, 26–27.

perceiving his neighbors superficially, failing to take the time and care to see them accurately.

Either mindset has political implications. The more we understand our neighbors to be fully human, to be invested in the welfare of their souls, the more we might advocate for a community-minded, just approach to arranging society. The more we look away from our neighbors, believing their fates to be entirely separate from our own—or even in direct competition—the more we would advocate for any societal arrangement that benefits us, no matter the cost. The two mindsets—the two ways of living—capture a dynamic that PBHA students have been discussing for decades.

PBHA alumni consistently describe how PBHA helped them get out of the "Harvard bubble" (an oft-repeated phrase that captures not just Harvard's literal iron gates, but the campus's sense of separation from the economic difficulties faced by much of the rest of the city), first by transporting them in vans to Boston neighborhoods, then by allowing them to build a sense of community with and loyalty to people in Roxbury, Mission Hill, Chinatown, and other communities. It would be easy for students to look away from the faces of their fellow-man, in Brooks's terminology, and rarely leave campus, let alone become invested in a local community. By contrast, PBHA students—along with other student activists and organizers—have been a part of movements to reform hiring practices for the formerly incarcerated in Boston, fought for increased funding for youth jobs, organized a Living Wage campaign for Harvard workers, and responded to local parent requests to form summer and after school programs. In other words, the House has served as a place for students build meaningful relationships and express solidarity with Cambridge and Boston communities, rather than look away.

In addition to articulating the ways in which service might be personally expansive, "The Beauty of a Life of Service" also includes an explicit call to action—a framing of *why* service is so urgently needed, and the material consequences of answering that call. Brooks acknowledges the overwhelming nature of inequality and poverty, and how frequently it can lead people to hopelessness. But it is the nature of service, he argues, to have unseen consequences; therefore, the impact of service cannot be underestimated. "Do not say in your terror, 'I will do nothing,'" he exhorts. "You must do something."[23] More than offer encouragement, Brooks declared the sheer fact of what could be done should enough privileged people concern

---

23. Brooks, *Addresses by the Right Reverend Phillips Brooks*, 34.

themselves with service: "There are men enough in this church this morning . . . to save this city, and to make this a glowing city of our Lord, to relieve its poverty . . . to touch all the difficult problems of how society and government ought to be organized then with a power with which they should yield their difficulty and open gradually."[24]

While plenty might offer a reasonable critique of any Harvard-associated person claiming to "save" Boston or Cambridge (either today or in the 1890s), the idea that the wealth and power concentrated in that institution ought rightfully be put to work to address social issues just across the river is a resonant one. PBHA students have wrestled with the possibilities and limits of this idea as well. Programs created in response to community need have provided support to thousands, but still raise questions of just how much one program can do when structural issues are at the root. But it is true that too many of the issues of inequality are seen as intractable when they might be addressed through different policies, budgets, and political priorities—particularly if Harvard students shaped by their PBHA experience carry those values forward if they pursue careers in those areas.

Brooks was addressing primarily Harvard students in that sermon, but today PBHA is also led by young people who have found their way to its programs in other ways. Just this summer, the Roxbury Youth Initiative (RYI) was directed by Aby Hansell, a former camper who grew up in the neighborhood. Her staff support person was Shaquanda Brown, another former camper who'd mentored Aby through her progression to counselor, then director. In the RYI universe, Harvard is important as a funder, and PBHA as a structural scaffolding and source of mentorship, institutional memory, and the administrative resources of a nonprofit. The relationships, neighborhood knowledge, connections, and community ties, however—in other words, the qualities that make a life-changing program—are in Roxbury. As PBHA seeks to center community voice in the development and leadership of its programs, its community of practice—now made up of staff, students (Harvard and otherwise), and program participants—can now make room for the wisdom and experience within the Boston and Cambridge community, to the benefit of all involved.

PBHA students frequently refer to the Summer Urban Program, a network of community-based summer camps run by students, as "the hardest summer you'll ever love." The work in this program and others is rarely easy, but frequently life-giving. Committed service requires many

---

24. Brooks, *Addresses by the Right Reverend Phillips Brooks*, 36.

hours a week of already-busy young people, often placing them in challenging or emotionally draining situations. Facing systems of oppression that leave people unhoused or undocumented is no small undertaking. But service and advocacy can still provide an answer to that "terror" Brooks spoke of—the fear and overwhelm that convinces people to do nothing. Doing *something*—whether that's tutoring a child or staging a sit-in in the Harvard president's office—not only provides an antidote to that paralysis, but provides an opportunity to find that "divine nature" which Brooks encouraged his listeners to seek in their neighbors. Seeking a life of service inevitably asks us to consider what is owed to our community, what difference we want to make with our time on earth, and what principles are more important to us than earthly concerns. Even when secular, they are unquestioningly spiritual.

Different challenges have arisen for each generation, challenging the identity of both PBHA and the students themselves. In 2020, PBHA faced major disruptions to its service model in the face of COVID-19. Would the organization have to abandon its services at a time when community members needed them most? How would the community of practice—generations of students, alumni, and staff—come together to respond? In the early days of figuring out the answers to those questions, staff and students began with one shared conviction: the knowledge that across generations, young people have been able to figure out solutions to some of the hardest problems, and so PBHA should allow them to do that now. Working together, they developed and clarified the principles and assumptions that would guide them through the next two years and enable them to provide some of their most urgent services through enormous challenges. Boston-area PBHA alumni, junior counselors, and students mobilized to deliver Chromebooks to local youth so that they could participate in virtual programming. Older alumni in the area provided housing to students unable to travel home when the campus closed. As they faced these challenges, a new generation wrestled once again with the question of their responsibility to the world, of what it meant to be in service of something larger than themselves.

At the opening of the House, Robert Treat Paine wished "that this memorial building may be clothed with power, in ways more mysterious than we mortals can understand, to impress the wondrous lesson of [Phillips' Brooks's] life on multitudes of the men who in these and future years shall enter its doors or only look upon its walls as they pass."[25] It is clear that

---

25. Paine, *Phillips Brooks House*.

many of those lessons have endured. They remain visible in the questions, community, solidarity, and commitment of today's students. That persistence of ideals may be less a mark of "ways more mysterious than we mortals can understand," but instead proof of how generations of students have wrestled with these enduring questions—proof of their urgency, their visceral and even spiritual nature.

BIBLIOGRAPHY

Brooks, Phillips. *Addresses by the Right Reverend Phillips Brooks*. Boston: Joseph Knight, 1894.
Brooks, Phillips. "Last Sermon Preached by Phillips Brooks in Appleton Chapel." *The Harvard Monthly* 15 (1893).
Clark, B. "A Sermon by Phillips Brooks on the Death of Abraham Lincoln." *Historical Magazine of the Protestant Episcopal Church* 49 (1980) 37–49.
Fallows, W. G. "The Jubilee of Phillips Brooks (1835–1893)." *The Modern Churchman* (1943).
Gips, Donald H. "Babbling Brooks: A History of the Phillips Brooks House Association." Harvard University Social Studies Thesis, March 1982.
Gotlieb, H. "The Friendship and the House: Phillips Brooks and Edwin Hale Abbot." *Historical Magazine of the Protestant Episcopal Church*, 32.1 (1963) 37–48.
Harp, G. "The Young Phillips Brooks: A Reassessment." *Journal of Ecclesiastical History* 48 (1998) 652–67.
Paine, Robert Treat. *Phillips Brooks House*. Address in Harvard Yard, 1900.

Afterword

The Rt. Rev. Phoebe A. Roaf

This book of essays about the life and legacy of Phillips Brooks, a late nineteenth-century Episcopal clergyperson, author, and public figure, serves as a testament to the transformative nature of being in a relationship with the living Lord. By examining the key influences in Brooks's life, the authors provide a glimpse into the formation of Brooks's opinions and character. The level of power and privilege he wielded as a Boston Brahmin in the early 1800s could have made him immune to the suffering of enslaved persons of African descent. Instead, his faith led him to champion an unpopular cause and to work on behalf of persons far removed from his social circle.

Brooks's life reminds us of the twists and turns in every individual's story. One helpful thing about reviewing another person's history is the invitation to reflect on our own journey. Considering the important moments in their lives, we can identify pivotal inflection points in our story. This experience was certainly the case for me as I read these essays. When I was invited to write the afterword for this book, I hadn't considered the similarity in our respective journeys. This exercise proved to be a trip down memory lane, given that Brooks and I are both alumni of Harvard College and Virginia Theological Seminary (VTS) and served as bishops. Although we are separated by time and demographic characteristics, many aspects of his life resonated with me.

This overview of Brooks's life starts with his upbringing. Elaine Flanagan explored his childhood and his mother's important role in his spiritual formation. The letters exchanged between Brooks and his mother attest to her ongoing influence throughout the course of his life. Christians in every generation have been nurtured in the faith by their mothers. St. Monica's fourth-century prayers for her son, St. Augustine of Hippo, are among many examples. Holy Scripture also gives us a sense of Mary's impact on her son Jesus' ministry. Brooks's childhood speaks to the significance of being raised in the church and having a praying mother. This is true irrespective of socioeconomic status, race, or culture. Being grounded in a life of faith took root and sustained Brooks throughout his life.

Brooks's Harvard College experience would have been customary for a young man of his social class. My first exposure to Brooks came when I was a Harvard undergraduate in the 1980s, 130 years after Brooks's graduation. One of my college jobs was serving at a Phillips Brooks House Association (PBHA) agency, a collection of student organizations focused on public service. I regularly passed the statute of Brooks during my time at PBHA and wanted to learn more about his life. It was not difficult to find materials outlining his work as a preacher and pastor in Boston and his efforts to end the institution of slavery. United States History was my undergraduate major, and I was intrigued by his legacy of service to others. It is fitting that Harvard named its primary public service initiative after him. Mary Catherine Curley's essay highlighted the ongoing impact of PBHA on both the students who work there and the community members who are served, and I can attest to this through personal experience.

Following a brief stint as a teacher, Brooks enrolled as a seminarian at VTS. His transition from Harvard College to VTS included the gamut of emotions experienced by generations of seminarians. Since 1823, VTS has formed laypersons and clergy for service in the Episcopal Church and the Anglican Communion. The seminary Brooks entered differed greatly from the community I joined in 2005, but VTS's primary purpose hasn't changed over time. Seminary comes from the Latin word *seminarium*, which means plant nursery or seed bed. The purpose of any seminary community is to nurture persons who seek to undertake ministry that will bear fruit. Part of the gardening process entails pruning and weeding the plants. The same is true of seminarians—through worship, study, and community engagement, a person is shaped to serve the church.

Brooks's VTS experience played a pivotal role in his formation. Even more important than the academic experience was his personal encounter with the institution of slavery in Virginia. Robert Flanagan describes how Brooks's upbringing and limited exposure to the South would have shielded him from the worst aspects of slavery. Understanding something from an

Afterword

academic perspective is one thing, but there's no substitute for firsthand experience. Brooks's time at VTS was instrumental in solidifying his opposition to slavery. The inhumane treatment he witnessed was in opposition to his understanding of the teachings of Jesus.

In recent years, VTS has examined its history and acknowledged the important contributions made by enslaved Africans and Black workers during Reconstruction and the Jim Crow era. This effort culminated in 2019 when VTS announced the creation of an endowment dedicated to the payment of reparations and the intent to continue researching and recognizing Black people who labored on the campus. VTS's reparation initiative also includes funds to support the work of Black congregations with significant ties to the seminary, to create programs that promote justice and inclusion, and to elevate the work and voices of Black alums and clergy within The Episcopal Church (TEC). You can learn more about this work on VTS's website (www.vts.edu). Additional resources about VTS's history include *No Turning Back: The Black Presence at Virginia Theological Seminary* by the Rev. Joseph M. Constant and *Grace in Motion: The Intersection of Women's Ordination and Virginia Theological Seminary* by Judith M. McDaniel.

Karen Swallow Prior's essay was instructive regarding Brooks's process of writing O Little Town of Bethlehem during the Civil War. His trip to the Holy Land led to the poem's creation, which would become a beloved hymn of the church. Brooks turned a painful experience into something life-giving for future generations, emblematic of the Christian journey.

Every clergyperson will acknowledge that the congregations we serve shape our vocation. Brooks's time in Philadelphia as a priest at the Church of the Advent and the Church of the Holy Trinity helped to develop his preaching and ministry. Rachel Wenner Gardner's essay adeptly explores the impact of those two congregations on Brooks's ministry. I imagine Philadelphia's role in our nation's history was also impactful for Brooks. Being near the place where the founding fathers crafted the Declaration of Independence, with its aspirational statement that all people have the right to life, liberty, and the pursuit of happiness, provided another incentive for Brooks to encourage his parishioners to embody these values.

During the Civil War, Brooks's sermons highlighted his opposition to slavery. His message, forcefully delivered by a tall figure, helped establish Brooks as a person of national prominence. Ruthanna Hooke explored Brooks's development as a preacher, highlighting his incorporation of the personal in his sermons and his concern for his listeners. Brooks was dedicated to his craft—while his first sermon was not memorable, he worked hard to identify an authentic style that conveyed his understanding of the Gospel.

After ten years in Philadelphia, Brooks returned to Boston in 1869 to become rector of Trinity Boston, where he served until becoming Bishop of the Diocese of Massachusetts in 1891. Robert Flanagan's chapter outlines the controversies associated with Brook's episcopate election. Brooks's commitment to ecumenism proved to be a challenge for some dioceses as they determined whether to vote in favor of his election. In the final analysis, Brooks did receive the consents necessary. Unfortunately, his episcopate only lasted fifteen months. In this sixth year of my episcopate, I wonder about his possible impact within TEC and the Anglican Communion had his tenure been longer. Given Brooks's eloquent advocacy for enslaved persons, his presence in the House of Bishops and at Lambeth Conferences could have been considerable. He died in 1893 in Boston, Massachusetts, when he was Bishop, so he never had the chance to enjoy retirement.

This afterword was written during the season of Advent, a time when we anticipate Christ's coming to the world in human form. We yearn for deliverance from the evils of the world through hope in the One who rules with righteousness, justice, and truth. And yet, God does not work in isolation. We are privileged to be co-creators with God in bringing about God's plan of salvation. That entails naming the evils of our day and working on behalf of vulnerable members of our community. There is much work to be done given the deep polarization within American society, an ecological system teetering on disaster, and the intractable nature of sexism, racism, and homophobia.

Brooks continues to be relevant because of his willingness to advocate for those less fortunate than himself. He was a pivotal figure in nineteenth-century American history, and his life serves as a reminder that one person can make a difference through the strength of their character. The Episcopal Church recognizes Brooks on January 23rd, the date of his death, as part of our commemoration of saints and occasions throughout the church year. The collect for his feast day summarizes his enduring legacy:

> Everlasting God, who implants your living Word in the minds and on the lips of all who proclaim your truth: Grant that we, like your pastor and preacher Phillips Brooks, might proclaim your Gospel in our own generation with grace and power. Through Jesus Christ our Lord, who lives and reigns with you and the Holy Spirit, ever one God, now and for ever. Amen.

www.ingramcontent.com/pod-product-compliance
Lightning Source LLC
Chambersburg PA
CBHW070911160426
43193CB00011B/1423